Stock Market Investing for Beginners: Day Trading + Swing Trading (2 Manuscripts)

The Complete Guide on How to Become a Profitable Investor. Includes, Options, Passive Income, Futures, and Forex

Adam Edwards

Table of Contents

Swing Trading For Beginners

Day Trading for Beginners

The Complete Guide on How to Become a Profitable Trader Using These Proven Day Trading Techniques and Strategies. Includes Stocks, Options, ETFs, Forex & Futures

Introduction

Before I begin, I want to thank you for purchasing this book as part of your trading research. I have spent a lot of time compiling some of the best sources from books to online resources in order to create one of the best beginner's guides for day traders.

This book is more than just a beginner's guide for anyone who wants to look into day trading. Not only will I discuss what day trading is, but I will also inform you of strategies, all the basics, the tools you will need, tips, how you can manage risk and much more!

In the first chapter, I will focus on what day trading is. Throughout this chapter, you will learn a few basic rules of day trading and the difference between trading and investing.

In the second chapter, I will talk about some of the basics you will look for when you start performing your trades. You will learn about what a watchlist is and what this list involves, how you need to have a trading plan you will stick to, and how to implement that plan.

There are a lot of different stocks when it comes to day trading. While it would be impossible for me to discuss all the different types of stocks you can take on as a day trader, I am going to take the time to discuss some of the most common stocks, such as penny stock and stocks in play in chapter three.

Chapter four is going to give you information about the platforms and tools that you will find as a day trader. Some of the tools involve preparation work before you become a trader, such as getting your education and building your business plan. In this chapter, I will also discuss the types of brokers you can look for along with your rights when it comes to working with your broker. From there, I will discuss a few different trading platforms to help give you an idea on what your broker might use or what you might want to install on your computer yourself.

Chapter five is going to focus on some of the tips and essentials that are important to note as a day trader. In this chapter, there are seven basic essentials, such as preparation, determination, finding a mentor, patience, and self-discipline that I will discuss in detail. From there, I will end the chapter with a few bonus tips for beginners. These tips come from experienced traders who wanted to give their advice on what you should do as a beginner.

Chapter six is going to dig a bit into the psychology of day trading as it focuses on the type of mindset you should have as you begin your day trading journey. Of course, it is important to note that it takes time in order to develop the right mindset--the *winning* mindset. I have broken down this chapter into the key characteristics that create the winning mindset and then ways to help you develop this state of mind.

Chapter seven is full of various trading techniques and strategies that you will find and use throughout your day trading career. For example, you will learn what the bull flag momentum and ABCD pattern strategies are. On top of this, I will also discuss trend following, spread trading, fading, range trading, and much more.

Chapter eight looks at some more basics that a beginner must know. This chapter focuses on various financial instruments that you can find as a day trader, such as stocks, currencies, futures, and ETFs.

Chapter nine is going to take a look at a type of day trading analysis known as fundamental analysis.

Chapter ten is going to look at another type of analysis, which is called technical analysis. In this chapter, I will explain what technical analysis is and how to use it.

Chapter eleven is going to take a look at how you can manage risk. Like any other trading, day trading carries risk, however, there are ways that you can limit risk so you can aim to gain the greatest profit possible. I will discuss the 1% rule, which is followed by the majority of day traders. I will also delve into common mistakes beginners make and how to avoid them.

Chapter twelve is going to give you a brief idea on what your day as a trader will look like, either as a full-time day trader or as someone who trades part time on the side. Both of these are discussed in this chapter, along with the downtime that the stock market sees around lunch and into the afternoon.

Chapter thirteen will list a variety of trading terms that you have read in this book or might find once you start trading. I wanted to include this in a glossary type setting so it could give you a way to easily look up a word that you are unsure about. One of the best ways you can become a successful day trader is to make sure that you understand the terminology of the profession.

My hope is that by the end of this book, you will feel confident about which route to take and what tools you need in order to become a successful day trader yourself. So, read on, get informed, and get started.

Chapter 1: What Is Day Trading?

Day trading is when people buy and sell stocks within a day. Some investors will buy in the morning and sell before the end of the day, while others will buy and sell throughout the day. The main strategies they use when investing are short-term. They are also known to use high leverage, which is using borrowed capital which can be used in any marketplace. Day trading has several positives and negatives, which will be discussed later in this book.

When you start trading, you will find that you can trade more than just stocks. In fact, you can trade money, options, and commodities. Some trades will be riskier than others. The type of trading you do will often depend on the type of risk you want to take on.

One of the biggest factors to keep in mind when it comes to day trading is if you hold a stock overnight, it is no longer day trading. Instead, this becomes *swing trading*. This is when you hold on to a stock for longer than a day, up to a few weeks. If you are more interested in swing trading, you will want to research this topic. You do not want to follow the tools or strategies discussed in this book if you are a swing trader. However, this doesn't mean that you can't be both a day trader and a swing trader. There are many investors who take part in both businesses. You just want to make sure you understand they are different forms of trading and use the right tools and strategies for each one.

It is very important as a day trader that you stick to your plans. There are always the moments that day traders have, even experienced ones, where they think they should hold onto the stocks overnight. Unfortunately, the end result of this is typically a larger loss in money. Of course, no one wants to lose money on any stock, which is often exactly why day traders will decide to hold their stocks overnight. Day traders feel that if they hold on to a certain stock, it will become less of a loss the next day. While there are a few stories of luck, these lucky moments rarely occur. Therefore, you will typically see less of a loss if you close out your positions at the end of the day.

Rules of Day Trading

Let's turn our focus to some of the rules of day trading that every investor should follow. These rules are not necessarily set in stone. You can decide to take these rules with you on your investing journey or ignore them. However, they should be followed in order to give you the best day trading experience from the very first day of your investing career.

Day Trading is a Serious Business

When some people start day trading, they think that it's meant to be fun and games and don't take the profession seriously. This can be a grave mistake. While you want to enjoy what you are doing, you always want to remember that it is a serious business.

There are some types of investing that are easier to handle as a side career or on the weekends. If this is the type of investing you are looking for, you will not want to look at day trading. This type of investing is meant to be a daily business and many people look at it as their day job. This means that once you decide to become a day trader officially, you need to treat it as you would any other career. You have to get up in the morning, get ready for your day, and make sure you are ready to work by your set time, which could be as early as 7 in the morning.

While you will have some flexibility in your schedule from a regular job, meaning you could set a bit of a later start time in the morning, you will want to make sure to set a schedule you will follow at least Monday through Friday. Even working from home, you will want to make sure to limit distractions. For example, you won't want to focus on day trading and watching television at the same time. Set up an office for yourself and pay attention to your work. Get ready for your job as a day trader like you would for your job at any other office. Don't head into your office in your pajamas. You're more likely to feel like you want to put in 100% effort and succeed if you treat this as a career.

Day Trading Will Not Help You Get Rich Quickly

You should *not* look at day trading as a get rich quick arrangement. This is a common misconception and one reason people often turn to day trading. If you truly want to become a successful day trader, you will need to make sure you not only have the patience to build your investments, but also realize it takes time.

Day Trader is Harder Than it Looks

Day trading is not as easy as it looks, but this does not mean that you should set this book down and decide not to become a day trader. It just means that you will probably need to spend more time learning about day trading than you initially thought. You want to make sure you are well-versed in the field before you make your first investment. Luckily for you, this is one of the reasons I decided to write this book. I want to give you a comprehensive beginner's guide so you can learn as much as you can about day trading to start your journey in one location. In other words, I have done most of the research for you.

Trading is Different from Investing

One of the biggest rules that you should understand before becoming a day trader is this is different from investing. In order to help you understand the difference, here are a few basic differences between trading and investing:

As an investor, you need to have an idea where the stocks are heading in the future. However, as a day trader, you only need to concern yourself with which stocks will give you the best financial gain on that day. You look more closely at the minutes. In fact, you won't even pay much attention to the hours and definitely won't worry about the next day, week, month, or year.

You Won't Win Every Trade

It does not matter how experienced you become as a day trader, there will still be days that you lose on a trade. Many people create an image in their mind where they will become so experienced at trading that they will never make a mistake and they will only gain capital. While this is a great vision to help keep your mindset positive (I will discuss this in chapter 6), you will continue to suffer a loss with some of your trades. The trick to help you lose as little capital as possible when you lose on a trade is to follow the various risk management strategies. I will discuss several risk management strategies later in this book.

Chapter 2: Basics of Performing a Trade

Now that you have a good idea of what day trading is and is not, I will go into the basics of performing a trade. This chapter isn't a step-by-step guide to perform your first trade. However, it does describe the main steps you should complete as a day trader. This chapter holds the basic information that you need to know before you arrive to your first day at your new job.

Build Up Your Watchlist

Your watchlist is going to become one of the first things you check in the morning. This list gives you a listing of potential stocks for you on that day. Your watchlist will be made up of dozens of trading tools which will help you make the best decisions possible during your trading day. On top of this, you can continue to observe specific companies to see if you would like to make trades in them at some point. This is a place where you will be able to see patterns within trades and receive up-to-date information about the stock market. Then, once you see that a stock is right where you want it, you can make your next move.

There are thousands of stocks within the market, which means that while you can scan the market as a whole, you will definitely miss a lot if you don't build up the best watchlist as a trader. This watchlist allows you to include the stocks you feel are the best so you can continue to watch them without having to scan the market and go through all the stocks you are not interested in as they never perform well.

Of course, building your watchlist is not as simple as it sounds. However, this doesn't mean that it's impossible or you won't be able to create the best watchlist for your career. It just means that you will need to put in effort, do your homework, and make sure that you understand the environment of the market. Once you reach this point, you will be able to develop the best watchlist for you.

How much effort you have to put into your watchlist will depend on if you are a full-time trader or part-time. If you decide to go the halftime route, you will be able to keep your watchlist simpler. You can get away with having a couple of stocks on your watchlist. However, if you are a committed full-time trader, you will at least want a watchlist that reaches a few more. On top of this, most full-timers will add a second watchlist. This one usually isn't bigger than their main watchlist, but they still put the same amount of effort into their additional list.

Must Have Properties

Before I get into building your watchlist, I want to talk about the three main properties that every watchlist must have.

1. Uniqueness

It is important to make sure that you developed your watchlist to suit your needs. It should have your individual stock market taste that will help you reach the level of success you desire. As a trader, it is important to follow your thoughts, goals, and beliefs. While you will ask for and listen to advice from other traders, you need to make sure you follow your *own* path. In other words, whenever it comes to your detailed plans, like your watchlist, you want to create it. You do not want to rely on anyone else to help you develop your unique list.

2. Repeatability

You want to make sure that whatever detailed plan you create as your watchlist, you are able to complete this every time you sit down to work. Whether you are a part-time or full-time trader, you want it to be consistent and stable so you can repeat your outlined steps every day you trade.

3. Be Realistic

This can become more of an issue for full-time traders than part-time traders. Because part-timers generally have another means of income, they don't always focus heavily on the amount of money their trades bring in. However, full-timers know they have to make a certain amount of money for their budget. Because they usually don't have another way to generate an income, they put more stress on their trades. This can lead to unrealistic expectations within their watchlist. For example, many traders state that it is unrealistic to think you can watch four stocks at one time. Each stock has a large amount of information you need to process, and our minds can only remember so much at a time. Therefore, you are more likely to make mistakes and suffer losses if you are unrealistic with how many stocks you can watch at one time.

You need to make sure that you can manage the workload you place on yourself. Furthermore, the more stressed you become because of your watchlist, the more likely you are to let your emotions start spiking, which can cause you to suffer losses. While you might have to play around with how many stocks you can watch at once, you will want to do this slowly. For example, start with one stock and then work your way up to two. If you find that you can easily manage two stocks, then go up to three. If you find that this is still manageable, but you are unsure if you could handle another stock, then stick with three. You need to stick with what you can manage and what you are comfortable with.

Criteria to Look for When Developing Your Watchlist

Below I will discuss a few guidelines that you should always keep in mind when you are evaluating a stock. These guidelines not only work for when you are thinking of adding a stock to your watchlist but also as you observe the stock from your watchlist.

1. Patterns

It is critical to know the patterns of a stock you are thinking of adding to your watchlist. Through the pattern, you can get a sense of where the stock sits in the market, when a good time to make your move to buy or sell would be, and if the stock is worth your time and effort. The more you watch the pattern of the stock, the easier it is to predict it. However, this doesn't mean that you will be correct every time. In a sense, being wrong here and there is really just a part of the job. But, you want to do what you can to decrease your risk of loss, and one way to do this is by noting the pattern of a stock.

2. Stock analysis

I won't get too much into detail about stock analysis because this will be discussed in depth later in the book. However, I will mention that there are two types of stock analysis. The first type is technical analysis and the second type is fundamental analysis. When you are looking for a stock to add to your watch list, it is important to make note of the stock's analysis. Through the analysis, you will be able to gain the most information about your stock, which is guaranteed to help you make your decision.

3. Amount of risk

You will always want to pay attention to the validity of the stock, which is the amount of risk it holds. You won't want to take on any stocks that are higher than the level of risk you allow yourself in your trading plan. This is especially important for beginners, as you are still learning the basics of trading, so you should *not* take any stocks that are high risk to start with.

What to Avoid in Your Watchlist

Just like there are criteria that you want to pay attention to when adding stocks to your watchlist, there are also things you want to avoid.

1. Do not add dozens of stocks

There are many investors, especially full-time traders, who feel the more stocks they place in their watchlist, the better change they have of making money. While this might be true for some experienced traders, other top traders state that this is a mistake. In fact, there are many traders such as Timothy Sykes who believe that you want to limit the stocks on your watchlist to a couple and no more than five. For Sykes, it depends on your experience as a trader. If you are just starting out, you will want to stick with one or two. However, if you have several years of experience and find that you can handle a couple more stocks, then you can increase your number.

2. Do not take on large trades

This is another important point if you are new to the trading career. You don't want to take on trades that are too large for you as you will find yourself making mistakes. There is no way that you can win every time as a trader. Therefore, it become more important to keep your trades small. Think of it this way: when you trade small, your loss is going to be small, but if you trade big your loss will also be larger. You want to keep your loss small as you can with any trade, as no matter how much you observe a stock's pattern, you can't predict the future.

Tips for Beginners

Because there are no hard rules for developing your watchlist, it is important to watch the criteria and avoid the factors I have previously discussed. However, in order to help you create and manage your first watchlist, here are a few helpful tips.

1. Stay in the now

You want to remember to remain present when you are managing your watchlist. While the historical patterns of a stock can be helpful, especially for investors, as a trader you want to pay attention to the current day. Therefore, the historical patterns aren't as important to you as they will be to others.

2. Keep your education at the top of your list

This will be said again and again throughout this book because it is so important. You want to make sure that you do your research and are educated as a day trader before you take on your new career. Furthermore, you are going to continue to learn and grow once you start your job. When you create your watchlist, your education is just as important as it is for any other part of your day trading business. If you need to do more research to get a better handle on your watchlist, take the time to do this.

3. Remember your previous watchlist

You are going to create different watchlists throughout your trading career. It is important that you take note about each one of your watchlists in your trading journal. You can always go back to a previous watchlist in order to help you develop a new watchlist.

Pay Strict Attention to Your Trading Plan

No matter how experienced or comfortable you become as a day trader, you always want to make sure you are paying attention to your trading plan. You will want to review your trading plan as often as you need to. In fact, some traders state that you should review it every day you sit down to make a trade. As I will discuss later, your trading plan will consist of three main parts: enter strategy, exit strategy, and stop-loss. Of course, you can make your trading plan as detailed as you feel the need to. You will want to create a plan that lays out your criteria for taking on a stock, your criteria for trading off or selling the stock, and then any plans on how you will limit loss if you find yourself in a bad trade.

Execute Your Plan of Action

Once you have developed your watchlist and reviewed your trading plan, you can then put your plans into action and begin your day. When you go in for a trade, you will want to make sure you follow your trading plan exactly as it states. If you find you need to make any changes to your plan, you can make this note for any future trades. It is important to stick to your plan because this will help you learn where your strengths and weaknesses are as a trader.

When is the Best Time to Make Your Decision?

One of the biggest questions you are probably asking yourself right now is when the best time to make the decision to take on a stock might be. While some of this will depend on what technique you are using and your own personal beliefs, the main reasons are probable movement and pricing. Like any trader, you want to receive the highest profit you can. Therefore, as you start to get into trading, you will find little tips and tricks within the patterns that will help you decide when to make your decision.

Your education will also help you when it comes to needing to make a decision. This is another reason why making sure you take trading classes, do your research, and get involved in online communities are so crucial. The knowledge you gain about day trading can come from all of these sources.

The key thing to remember is that you do *not* want to hold the stock overnight. You want to make sure that you close it out by the end of the day. However, once you take on a stock you never truly know if you are going to trade the stock within five minutes or at the end of the day because you have to. This is why taking the time to analyze the stocks before you decide to put them into your list will help decrease risks and give you a better chance of making a capital gain.

Chapter 3: Finding a Suitable

Market

Once you get started trading stocks you will hear the phrase, "you are only as good as the stocks that you trade" often. According to many day trading experts, there is a lot of truth to this phrase. However, this phrase should not scare you away from day trading. Every beginner is unaware of what the best stocks are for their business at first. I want to help you learn what the best stocks are so you can get the best experience out of your day trading business from the beginning.

This is not to say that you aren't going to make mistakes. However, you shouldn't dwell on the mistakes you make in your business. Instead, you want to *learn* from them so you can step into the future of your day trading business with more experience and a lesson learned. You should also remember that even some of the most experienced day traders make mistakes. But, the more you take the time to learn about your new career, the fewer mistakes you will make along the way.

Just like any job, you want to make money consistently. Therefore, you need to pick stocks that are going to move and have enough volume. If you don't focus on these stocks, then you have wasted a trading day, made very little money, or even lost money.

Selecting the Best Stocks to Trade

Selecting the right stocks for your trades can be some of the toughest decisions you will make throughout your day. You will start this process right away in the morning as you catch up on the news and see what has changed in the stock market overnight. You will use your education, techniques, and other knowledge to go through and find a few stocks that pique your interest as a possible trade that day.

One of the most important factors to remember before you select is that you want to make sure you believe this stock is going to give you a sizable profit. Think of it this way: you can purchase a stock for $15 and then within five minutes sell the stock with a profit of $500. For many people, this is more money than they make in their usual day job in one day and you just made it within five minutes.

While this example isn't how most of your trades will happen, it is possible. You just have to make sure that you follow the steps, learn as much as you can, and follow the basics that are written in this book and elsewhere about day trading. You will also want to realize that you will not become a success overnight. In fact, it can take months before you start to see a good profit.

But still, this does not answer what type of stocks you can select as a day trader. While I can't tell you what specific stocks will be best for you (as only you can decide that), I can give you a brief list of some of the stocks you will run into as a day trader that seem to be on the popular lists.

Penny Stocks

Penny stocks are an option you can consider. These stocks are not very popular and they tend to be a part of the market where most day traders don't look. However, these stocks are some of the cheapest to buy, and although they are typically over a penny, they tend to be under $1 each. At the same time, many of these stocks tend to not trade for more than $5. This can still give you a good profit if you invest in the right penny stocks. The trick is understanding the details of penny stocks in order to gain the best profit from them.

At the same time, penny stocks can give you a large capital loss. This is because the companies that go in the penny stocks category are the ones who aren't doing the best and hope to make some money through investments made in their company. This can often work out better for the company than it does the trader, mostly because the company will gain the money you put into the stock, whereas you could end up losing money on your trade.

Because of this, you want to make sure you understand what company you are purchasing from if you decide to get into penny stocks. If you know how to handle penny stocks and the company seems to be on the more successful side, then you are more likely to gain a profit than receive a loss. However, it is not just the company you want to become aware of when if you trade in penny stocks.

You also want to make sure that you know where you heard about the penny stocks. Unfortunately, like other areas in the world, the stock market is full of people who are trying to scam other people out of money one way or another. Some of these people will focus on penny stocks. They will purchase tons of penny stocks and then make fake news releases or post untrue information about how well the company of the penny stock is doing. They will talk about how if you purchase some of these stocks you will be able to end your day with a huge profit. However, because there is no hard truth in what they are saying, you could well end up with a loss at the end of the day instead of a profit. This is another reason why it is extremely important to make sure you do your research before you take on any stock or other investment.

Stocks in Play

This is a popular phrase that day trader often use. Stocks in play refer to stocks which have great reward opportunities. However, because of this, they can also have higher risk than other stocks. Due to this, it is best that beginners gain a little trading experience before they start looking at stocks in play.

Stocks in play will change daily, which tends to be a benefit for day traders. All the stocks included in stocks in play allow you to become efficient with your buying power, which is one of the best ways to earn a profit.

How can you find stocks in play? There are actually several avenues that allow you to find stocks that are included in this category. For example, stocks that have fresh news, a stock that has increased or decreased around 2% right before the market opened for the day, or a stock that has great intraday levels.

SPDR S&P 500 ETF

The SPDR is one of the hottest stocks on the market in 2019. Whether you are more interested in investing or you are a day trader, this is a common stock to see. When it comes to trading, the SPDR receives over 100 million trades a day, and it is known to generate pretty good profits.

While this might seem like the right investment for a day trader as many people feel it almost guarantees a profit, you still want to make sure that it fits in with your strategy. On top of this, you will want to follow your trading plan before purchasing this stock. Even if the stock is known as one of the most popular stocks with good profit, you will still want to make sure it fits your plan, your strategy, and your style as a trader.

Successful Companies Often Mean Popular Day Trade Stocks

Some of the most common stocks people look at as day traders are also some of the most popular companies. For example, JCPenney, Facebook, and Yahoo! often top the lists. While these stocks are popular because of the benefits and gains that day traders tend to receive from them, this doesn't mean that you want to jump on these stocks to start with. As stated before, you want to make sure that it fits into your plan, strategy, and every other facet of your trading scheme before you decide to take on any of the more popular stocks.

On top of this, for day traders, some of the most popular companies can also have larger risks than other companies. Because of this, you are going to want to make sure that the stock fits into your level of risk before you make any type of purchase or trade.

Factors to Help You Select the Best Stocks

In order to help you find the best stocks for yourself, you need to first develop your trading plan. This is the plan you will follow throughout your career. You will also review this plan often. This plan will be discussed later in this book in greater detail.

Another developmental step you will want to focus on before you dive into the market is to make sure that you have chosen your strategy and you have a thorough understanding your strategy. You need to make sure that you know your strategy well, because you will often have to quickly think when it comes to analyzing a stock and whether it will work with your strategy or not.

Once you get through the basics of starting up your trading business, then you can start focusing on what type of stocks you will look for. While I have discussed a few stocks and information about what type of stocks many day traders look at above, I also want to discuss the several factors that can aid you in deciding which stock is best for you.

Volatility and Volume

Volatility is a mathematical measurement that you will want to complete in order to help you determine what types of returns you will receive from a specific stock. One of the keys rules to remember when it comes to volatility is the higher the measurement, the riskier the stock will be.

When we discuss volume in the stock market, we are referring to the number of shares that were traded throughout the day. You will pay a lot of attention to volume when you get into the technical analysis part of your day trading career.

Both volume and volatility are important when you are looking for what type of stock to watch to see if it is something you will be interested in purchasing or trading. Of course, you will always want to watch the guidelines and factors that you set for yourself in your business plan, such as your risk level and the amount of volume you feel comfortable with.

If you are a trader who is more interested in your stock moving slowly, then you will want to focus on stocks that have higher volume than volatility. However, if you want to focus on stocks where the prices tend to increase and decrease rapidly, then you will look in another direction when picking your stock.

It is important to note that no matter what stock you are looking at, volatility and volume are going to change over time. This is a natural process of the trading world and one that you will become used to. In fact, it is through these two factors that you will begin analyzing the stocks you are looking at to gauge your interest level in taking on these stocks.

Social Media

It seems that we are officially living in a world where no matter what profession we become a part of, social media is going to show up somewhere along the line. This is no different in the day trading profession. You will review social media often from the different stocks you can pick from, such as Instagram, Facebook, and Twitter to find a place to get some of the current news about the stock market.

However, there are many day traders who state that you have to be cautious when you are looking at social media to help you pick your next stock. If you have ever paid attention to the news reports that you see on Facebook, you might have come to the realization that not all of these reports are based on facts. The unfortunate part the increase in social media is that anyone can publish anything and get it trending in social media news. Because of this, you could find yourself reading a report that doesn't speak the whole truth. This is why you should always make sure to find more than one source that states the same thing when it comes to news reports about the stock market.

Look for Stocks Which Show an Upward Swing

Some day traders say what helps them find the best stocks is to find one that has slowly increased in price over time. You will be able to see this trend when you are focusing on the technical analysis part of stock trading, as this is when you look through the history of the stock.

Of course, you want to keep in mind that this might not be the best factor for you to focus on. For example, if you follow a technique which tends to focus on making a trade when you see the stock price decrease during the day, you might find stocks that have been increasing slowly are not the best fit. However, it is also important to remember that stock prices go up and down during the day. Therefore, even a stock which has shown to go up gradually will have moments throughout the day where the price drops.

Chapter 4: Tools and Platforms

Get Your Education

You need to make sure you are educated on your topic. You want to treat day trading as your new career. Therefore, you should make sure that you have researched your topic and consider yourself an expert on day trading. Of course, there are lessons that you are going to learn naturally as you start day trading. Experienced traders believe that people should take about three to four months and practice with simulators before practicing with money.

Build Your Business Plan

You need to have a business plan. One of the biggest factors to remember when you are getting into day trading is you have to treat it like any other serious career choice. With any business you would start up and get into, you will have a business plan. You need to make sure your education is part of your business plan (for example, any classes you are planning on taking). You also have to make sure your schedule, the tools you will use, platforms, technology, software, and anything else incorporated in your business is a part of your business plan.

Another thing to remember when creating your business plan is to look at every single detail. You do not want to miss something or think it is fine to skip over anything. On top of this, you want to make sure that you look at your business plan often, even after you start trading. In fact, it is best if you look at your business plan at least once a month, if not more.

Make Sure You Have the Right Supplies

You will want to make sure that you find a system of support from a community of traders, have high-speed internet service, a great platform which supports hotkeys, a scanner which will help you find the right stocks to trade, and the best broker. You will also want to make sure that you can financially handle the bills that will become a part of your new day trading career. These bills can include leases and licenses for software, your monthly internet bill, electricity bill, your broker's commission, and any platform costs. Furthermore, you will probably want to become a part of an online community, a practice that has several benefits I will discuss later in his book, and bear in mind that these communities often have subscriptions.

Have Enough Cash

You will need to make sure that you have enough cash, which is often referred to as startup capital. Similar to any other business, you will want to make sure you can afford to take on day trading. However, you will not only need money when you start investing, you will also need money to make sure that you can afford the bills and technology that goes into day trading, as mentioned earlier.

Making sure you have enough finances is an important step because one of the main reasons why most day traders lose their money or go bankrupt is because they didn't have enough startup capital. If you need to hold off on starting up your day trading career for a couple of months or more in order to make sure you have enough capital, that is okay. As the old saying goes, it is better to be safe than sorry. You don't want to find yourself thinking of ways to cut back in order to save your money for investing. For example, it is a bad idea to decide not to go forth with any classes or day-trading community subscriptions over financial concerns, as these are incredibly important. If you start cutting back on the tools that can help you become a successful day trader, you can easily find yourself in a downward spiral. This can cause you not only to lose more money but also cause you a lot of stress and emotions within trading, which can cause more problems within your investing career by impairing your ability to make quick decisions based on logical analysis. If you are not prepared, you are more likely to make mistakes.

Find a Broker

One of the first things you will want to do is to find a trusted broker. It is important that you not only find a capable, competent broker but one whom you can trust. Remember, you will be getting assistance from your broker about your financial future. Therefore, you will want to make sure that you not only talk to the broker before you agree to hire, but you will also want to take extra steps in checking into your broker's background. You have the right to find out how your broker has handled other people's accounts. For example, background information can tell you about any complaints people have filed against the broker previously. On top of this, you will be able to see your broker's employment history and get an idea of why the broker changed jobs in the past.

The broker you pick will help you with many tasks. Not only with they give you advice on which stocks to pick but they might also go through with the buying and selling process of the stocks. The best brokers will work with you and help you learn the trade. If you find that your broker is withholding information of any type, such as not giving you the correct information about stocks or not allowing you to see your records, you need to find a different broker. You always have the right to see all your records and know exactly what your broker is doing with your stocks and finances.

Know Your Rights

Before you search for your trusted broker, there are several pieces of information you should know first. One of these is your rights when it comes to working with a broker.

- You have the right to ask for and receive information about your broker's background. This can help you get to know your broker, so you can find one that you can trust with your personal information and finances.

- You have the right to know all the information about any stocks or trades before your broker makes any purchase or sale.

- You have the right to all reports about your trading.

- You have the right to ask any questions or seek any other means to help you understand all the reports and information you are given.

- You have the right to receive all forms of communication in the form of letters or other means of written correspondence. No one has any right to keep you from seeing and understanding any of your information.

- If you do not feel that you are receiving all your information, you do not understand your reports, or you do not feel your broker is helping, you have the right to go above your broker to his or her supervisor.

- If your broker is part of a branch firm, you have the right to go to the branch firm's headquarters with any questions or concerns.

- You have the right to contact your state or county agency with any concerns about your broker's background, including employment history or any complaints filed against your broker.

Types of Brokers

1. Sure Trader is a broker who focuses on international trades. Sure Traders also tend to focus on helping the day traders who do not fall under the $25,000 minimum rule for United States residents. This rule is known as the pattern day trader rule set up by the Financial Industry Regulatory Authority. This rule states that not only must the day trader maintain a $25,000 minimum balance in his account, but the customer must also make at least four trades during a five day period.

While Sure Traders are common for day traders, not all traders, especially when they first begin trading, can hold the minimum amount in their account. It is also important to note that these brokers have higher fees. For example, their commissions are usually higher, such as charging over $10 for one buy and sell trade. At the same time, Sure Traders are the best choice for people who cannot keep the minimum balance in their accounts.

2. Interactive Brokers tend to be one of the cheapest types of brokers, as they only charge about $1 per trade. However, they generally won't work with people who can't follow the pattern day trader rule. If you are a day trader who is planning on purchasing thousands of shares, this is the best type of broker for you because their fees are the lowest. However, you will want to make sure that you can follow the rule and have some experience in day trading. The more stocks you purchase, the more experienced you should be. It is fine to just start with a few stocks while you are still learning the ropes of day trading. This will help you limit mistakes and minimize risk. The more stocks you purchase, the more risk you have.

No matter what your conditions are, you always need to make sure that you find the right broker for you. Furthermore, you have to make sure that you can trust your broker. If you don't have a good relationship with your broker or you find yourself wondering if your broker is really helping you, it is time to take whatever steps you need to in order to secure your financial future.

Trading Platforms

There are a variety of trading platforms that you can use. You will want to make sure that you do your research on which platform is the best fit for you, whether it's through your broker or yourself. For example, if you find out through your research that your broker has an old platform which is slow, you won't want to choose that broker. You want to make sure that whatever platform you and your broker use, it is up-to-date and quick. If you have a platform that runs slower than most, you won't be able to make the trades correctly. Trades need to be done quickly in day trading. You generally want to trade as soon as you see a rise in your stock's price. If you are using a slow platform, your trade will not go through as it should and you can find yourself losing a lot of money. Below are several platforms that you can look into as you start your day trading journey.

DAS Trader

The DAS trader platform is one of the most popular platforms due to all the tools and services that the platform offers. On top of this, the platform has been around for nearly two decades and the developers have worked hard to make sure the technology within the platform stays up to date so traders can continue to have the best experience possible.

This platform likes to give traders the advantage to not only use the tools included in the platform, but also allows traders to learn strategies that can help take them to the next level as a trader. While many platforms focus on this, the DAS trader is known to offer this type of help for a trader at any level.

There are many stockbrokers who will focus on the DAS trading platform. Therefore, if you are interested in using this platform for your trading needs, you will easily be able to find a company or a broker that will not only use this platform but help you understand the platform as well.

Some of the services that the DAS trading platform has within its system are multiple stop types, a support for multiple monitors, real-time account management, and options and equities trading.

Trader Workstation (TWS)

While the general reviews for the TWS state that this is one of the best trading platforms available, there are other traders who say the platform can be difficult to navigate, at least at first. Many traders like this platform because of all the great tools and services it offers, from alerts to chart comparisons. Of course, these services are typically a part of every decent platform, however, the layout that comes with all these services tends to be very attractive for many traders.

Furthermore, this is another trading software which has been around awhile and continues to update. Many people state that with every update, there are bigger and better improvements for the TWS platform.

Lightspeed Trader

Lightspeed was released in 2006 and has since become one of the most popular platforms for traders. This platform offers a variety of services similar to the other platforms, with the added bonus of being able to customize your platform the way you want to see it. On top of this, Lightspeed Trader is known to be easy to navigate and easy to understand. In fact, many traders believe that this is an ideal platform for any beginner.

Chapter 5: Seven Essentials for Day Trading

When you are first starting your new career, you can never learn enough tricks and tips to help you become a successful day trader. This chapter will not only give you the seven essential tips that every trader needs to know but it will also include a bonus section with extra tips to help you start your day trading career.

The Seven Essentials

One of the most important essentials for any day trader is the right mindset. This essential is considered the foundation for your business. However, this does not take away the importance of the other essentials for day trading.

In the next chapter, I will discuss one of the most important essentials for any day trader, which is the right mindset. This essential received its own chapter because it is really the most important essential as it is considered the foundation for your business. However, this does not take away the important of the other vital elements of day trading.

1. *Education and simulated trading*

Education is an important part of your life no matter where you're heading in your chosen career. Education is also one of the most important steps for someone going into day trading.

For day trading, education is continuous. It doesn't matter if you are starting out in the field or if you are an experience day trader, you will always be working on research, learning everything you can about trading, and taking various day-trading courses.

For those interested in upping the ante when it comes to educating themselves on day trading by taking courses, there are three factors that you need to pay attention to when you are choosing your school.

1. Find a Mentor

You want to find a school where you know you can find a mentor. There are several reasons for this. First, you want to be able to go to this person for advice on day trading. Therefore, you should make sure that the instructor is not only trustworthy but also has great experience as a day trader. Second, it is hard to find your own mistakes. Therefore, you want to find a mentor who is going to be able to identify your mistakes and help you fix them so you can become the best day trader possible. Third, sometimes it is hard for us to see what we are doing correctly. We might think that we aren't doing something right, when in fact, we are doing great. Your mentor will also be able to point out your strengths and help you develop these assets even more.

2. Foundation

When you are looking for a course to take, you will want to find one that will teach you the various strategies and focus on other areas of day trading so you can receive a well-rounded education. There are several day trading schools online that allow you to view the strategies they teach for free, as this is a very important aspect of becoming a successful day trader.

3. Support

You will also want to find a school that offers the benefit of support *after* you complete the course. If you have ever graduated with your undergraduate, master's, or Ph.D., you will know how helpful support is after you have completed the program. This system of support can become a mentor to you once you have finished the course and are on your way to becoming a successful day trader. Another reason support is so important is because it is easy to forget the good habits and grab ahold of bad habits. Typically, you don't even realize this change yourself and someone else has to point it to you. Then, depending on how long you were focused on the bad habits, it could be really difficult for you to change these habits.

The popular online investing encyclopedia website known as Investopedia created a day trading course in 2017. The "Become a Day Trader" course covers everything you need to know from the beginning where you create a trading place to making your first trade. The course is taught by a 30-year veteran of Wall Street, David Green, who now wants to focus on helping day traders become more successful. Green was able to retire as a trader himself by the age of 40 due to his success. This course is about $200 and includes about 50 video lessons.

The Stock Whisperer is another site which has various day trading courses to help you reach your highest potential as a trader. Stefanie Kammerman is the creator of this site and not only has videos to help you learn but has also published books. Kammerman's trading career started in the mid-1990s and by 2010, she had created an online course to help other traders get their start in a new career. The courses range from $100 to $500 and offers support for after you start your career, provided you want the support Kammerman offers.

The Online Trading Academy is one of the most popular trading schools online. The academy started in 1997 with stock market courses and has grown to include various courses that focus on the stock market. In 2001, the

Online Trading Academy created a physical location for traders. Today, there are over 250,000 traders who are a part of the academy. Not only do they get to begin their trading career through the academy's courses, but they can also continue their education and gain support after starting their trading career.

You should also further your education by continuing your research. Even though I created this book to give you the best condensed beginner's guide I could, this doesn't mean that it should be the only book you read. There are a variety of other books on the topic that are just as important for you to reference in your career. Some of these books I have used as research myself when creating this book, while others I have found in order to give you a reading list. Here are a few books for you to take a look at:

1. Trading: Technical Analysis Masterclass: Master the Financial Markets by Rolf Schlotmann and Moritz Czubatinski received publication in 2019. This book focuses on the technical analysis portion of the stock market. However, the book also looks beyond technical analysis and into the psyche of the trader.

2. How to Day Trade for a Living: Tools, Tactics, Money Management, Discipline and Trading Psychology by Andrew Aziz. This book was published in 2015 and is known to be one of the most popular books on the

market. It gives you a variety of information on day trading from start to finish.

3. Advanced Techniques in Day Trading: A Practical Guide to High Probability Day Trading Strategies and Methods by Andrew Aziz received publication in 2018. This is Aziz's follow-up to his 2015 day trading book.

4. Day Trading: A Comprehensive Beginner's Guide to get started and learn Day Trading from A-Z by John Reigner received publication in 2019. This is another beginner's guide that gives you all the essential information you need in order to start your new career.

5. Day Trading Options: This Book Includes- Day Trading Strategies, Options Trading: Strategy Guide For Beginners, Trading Options: Advanced Trading Strategies and Techniques by Brandon Lee. This is a series of three books that received publication in 2018 and holds information for both beginners and advanced day traders.

Simulator trading is what you should always start trading with. You never want to start with real money as you will find, like every beginner trader does, that you make most of your mistakes at the beginning. Therefore, if you start with simulated trading, you won't have to worry about losing real money. This trading allows you to do trades in real time as practice. While some brokers will allow you to use previous market data, you want to use real-time market data.

Simulation trading is done using a software which you will have to pay for, usually on a monthly basis. For example, if you decide to use this software for about 5 months, you could pay around $600 by the end of your simulation trading education. While this might seem like a lot of money, it is completely worth it as you are able to learn the stock market hands-on without having to worry about losing any money. You will be able to gain a sense of your strengths, make mistakes, and learn how to fix those mistakes.

Experienced day traders who started with simulation trading state that this step is what kept them in the game. In fact, many previous day traders who didn't take this step first ended up leaving the business because they felt they were losing too much money and wouldn't be able to reach success as a day trader.

2. Preparation

Preparation is essential for any career path you take in life. Sometimes your preparation come in terms of education, such as day trading, becoming a doctor, or a teacher. Other times your preparations comes in forms of hands-on experience. When you prepare yourself to become a day trader, you will use both of these forms of preparation. However, there are other preparatory measures that you will take throughout your career.

These are:

1. The morning preparation before the stock market opens, which will be discussed in-depth later in this book.

2. The research you must collect before you make a trade.

Once you start to get into the day trading career, you will find that the earlier you get up, the more time you have to prepare for your day. Not only will you be able to take your time to get ready and eat breakfast, but you will also be able to take time to read the news and catch up on the changes of the stock market. This can help you become more successful as a day trader. On top of this, you will feel less rushed in the morning, which will allow you to keep a level head and keep your emotions out of your decisions.

Many experienced day traders say they often miss good stocks if they don't take the time they need in the morning to scan the stock market, the news, and pick their top stocks for the day. On top of this, more time is going to allow you to talk to your mentor or gain advice from members of your online community. There are many experienced traders who want to help beginner traders and because they realize how the day goes, they will be in the online community early the morning to offer any advice.

3. Determination

The determination you have for your day trading job is going to be different than the determination people have for other professional careers. For example, there are several careers where you could work 60 or more hours a week. This is not something you want to do as a day trader. You want to keep your schedule to between 40 to 50 hours a week. Of course, you will have the hours the stock market is open and any hours you spend preparing for your day or analyzing your day after the market closes.

Day traders work hard. They are not just staring at their computer screens waiting for the next big profit. They are constantly thinking critically about their next steps and asking a series of questions throughout the day. Some of these questions include:

- Is this stock moving quickly or slowly?

- What type of pattern is this stock showing?

- What is the best strategy for this stock?

- Is this stock going to give me a good profit?

- What is the risk level of this stock?

- Is the seller or buyer in control of the price?

- Is this stock weaker or stronger than the market?

These questions are being asked by day traders before they make any type of decision on whether they will take the next step towards the stock.

In order to help yourself remain determined to work hard and do your best as a day trader, it is important that you make sure this is the career you absolutely want. Of course, you can always walk away from the business if you find it isn't what you thought it would be, however, you could lose thousands of dollars doing this. Therefore, it is best to just know that this is the right direction for you before you pick up your first stock.

Another way to help yourself stay determined is to make sure you are educated, have a foundation, and a system of support. These factors, which I discussed earlier, will help you when it comes to your mental stability as a day trader. It is very important to make sure that you are happy in your career and don't feel any more stress than you have to. If you lose your healthy mental stability for your job, you will start to find you're making decisions based on your emotions, which can make you not only lose interest in your job, but begin to make avoidable mistakes that cost you money.

Making sure you have a daily routine that you follow will help you remain determined to become the best day trader you can be. A routine will not only help you keep track of all your reports, your journaling, and everything else but you will also help you be able to maintain a healthy mental attitude towards your career. Make sure to contact your mentor or support system in the morning and throughout the day if you have to. And, if you find yourself needing a mental break, then turn off your computer and take a mini vacation. Everyone needs a vacation from their careers now and then. However, you do not want to make a regular habit of this.

You also don't want to make a habit of getting too comfortable and deciding that because you are working from home, you can watch a movie in the middle of the day. While this is fine is you really need a mental break, you should on do this on rare occasions. It is easy for people to become distracted in their homes as they have music, television, game systems, and so much more at hand ready to steal their attention. But, in order to remain determined to work hard and do your best, you need to maintain your work schedule. You have to set up an area in your home where you are away from any distractions and can focus on your work. If worse comes to worst and you start realizing that you can't work from home, you might want to look into renting an office close to home or in an office building. Of course, this will cost money, which you will have to factor into your bills.

4. Patience

Patience is an important part of day trading. You will need to have patience for the career from the time you decide that you want to take part in this journey to the day you retire or quit.

It is important to note that you will not become profitable overnight. It might take months before you start seeing money rolling in at a comfortable rate. On top of this, if you want to become so successful that you can retire early, this can take years. Many day traders who have found that they could retire and live comfortably were in the career for 20 to 30 years before they did so.

You also want to remember that nearly every day trader, including the experienced ones who became successful, wanted to quit the job within the first few months. In fact, for many people, this was almost a daily thought in their mind. They would ask themselves if they had made the right decision or if they can become profitable as a day trader. You won't be any different. These thoughts are a part of every day trader's mind for at least the first few months. This is also a time where you are going to want to focus on your patience. You are going to want the patience to make sure you won't leave the job because of a few struggles, dozens of bad trades, or the process of adapting during the first few months.

You will also need the patience to watch the stocks. You don't want to just up and take on a stock without doing your research and watching for a pattern. Sometimes, this will mean that you spend a couple of hours paying attention to the stock. As a day trader, you want to make sure that you wait for the right stock and the right time to make a move. This requires a lot of patience and time.

5. Self-discipline

There is not only a lot of education and gaining of skills that go into learning to be a successful day trader, but also self-discipline. For example, it will take self-discipline to make sure that you are following your daily schedule, that you aren't playing video games or watching television when you should be working, or even just to be patient. While the techniques you will use as a day trader and the education you will receive are easy to understand, there are still difficult areas of day trading and one of these is self-control.

Before you truly get started in you day trading career, you will want to make sure that you have the self-discipline it takes to complete the tasks you will need to complete. This is something that you will want to start working on right away and continue to work on throughout your career. While it will always be something you work to improve, you will find that the more self-control you have, the easier your job becomes.

Everyone struggles with self-discipline now and then. Even experienced day traders have discussed how they struggled with self-control and had to work on various techniques to help build their self-discipline. Below are a few techniques which can help you build your self-discipline:

1. Remove any temptations in your area. This includes any technology or other distractions that can cause you to lose interest in your work and focus on something you shouldn't during your work day. For example, if you find yourself checking your cell phone often and it's decreasing your productivity at work, you can put your phone on silent or turn it off and place it out of your sight. When it comes to removing temptations, the phrase "out of sight, out of mind" really does ring true.

2. Believe in yourself, as this will help you change your willpower. Many times people tend to lack self-discipline because they don't believe that they can accomplish a given task. Because of this, they are less willing to put forth the effort it takes to make sure the task gets completed. However, once you start to change your perceptions of how well you do in your career, you will find that you are more determined to succeed. This can help increase your self-control because you want to do better and therefore, you will be more willing to focus on the tasks you need to.

3. Creating new simple habits can help you increase your self-discipline. Sometimes people lack control because they feel that establishing this new habit can be intimidating. This makes people feel that they won't be successful in the task which makes them back away from the good habit they are trying to form. In order to move past the feeling of a new habit becoming intimidating, it's easiest to break the habit into a series of small, easily digestible steps which can be accomplished one by one.

4. You want to make sure to build your self-discipline daily. Just like any other behavior, self-discipline is learned. Therefore, it is something that you will want to work on regularly, especially if you are trying to improve it. If you continue to work on building your willpower on a daily basis, it will soon become more automatic and remain a part of your mindset throughout the day.

5. Creating a backup plan can help increase your self-discipline. For example, if you find yourself struggling to get up early in the morning so you have enough time to get your research and news in before your work day, you can focus on a backup plan the night before. You could decide that instead of having your alarm clock right next to your bed, you set it across the room. Therefore, you have to get up in order to shut the alarm clock off.

6. Another tip to help you build your self-control is to make sure that you forgive yourself for any mistakes and

then move forward. This means that if your backup plan fails, you don't dwell on the fact that you didn't follow through with your backup plan. Instead, you tell yourself that you will do better next time and move on. This is also important when it comes to making bad trades. As a day trader, you have to realize that bad trades happen. You should note any mistakes and learn from them but not dwell on the fact you lost money. You need to learn from your mistakes and move forward with the added knowledge to help you in the future.

6. Mentorship and a community of traders

Joining an online forum or community is a great way to help you manage risk. Not only can you gain insight from other day traders, but you will be able to become a part of a community that shares your same interests. In a way, you can look at the people you get to know as your co-workers. Even though day trading is a competitive market, other day traders don't want to see anyone lose money. They want people to become successful. Therefore, most are ready and willing to help a beginner.

There are a variety of online communities that you can choose from. While I won't list them all here, below are a few of the most popular ones.

1. The Baby Pips Forum

This forum is the best for people who are new to the trading career. There are areas where you can post any questions you can have and maybe find a mentor to help you through your career. There is a lot of information about trading that you can learn from this forum.

2. Investors Underground

Nathan Michaud is the creator of the Investors Underground site, which is considered to be one of the top investing chat rooms for 2019. Starting in 2008, this chat room has over 100,000 members with most of them being more experienced traders. Like most pro traders, they are willing to do whatever they can in order to help beginners to become successful.

3. Timothy Sykes Chat Room

One of the most well-known day traders of 2019 is Timothy Sykes. He runs a great website with dozens of helpful articles for a day trader at any point of their career. On top of this, the website also has a forum where people can discuss any questions they have, seek advice, or receive other helpful information. This site is great for new traders and run by experienced day traders.

7. Record-keeping

Another section of this book will discuss record keeping as a day trader in more detail. However, this is also one of the most essential tips that you will need to follow throughout your career. Not only is it important to keep track of all your broker records and correspondence, but you should also start to keep a trading journal. While I will discuss more on this later, I will take this time to touch on some of the things you should track in your journal.

- What the time of the day you completed all your trades.

- What your physical and mental well-being was like that day. For example, did you get enough sleep, how were you feeling, were you distracted during your day, etc.

- What strategies you used during that day.

- What risks and rewards did you find from your trade?

- How did you find out about the trade?

- How did you manage your trade?

- What was the size of your trade?

- What was closing out for your day like?

Of course, you can write anything else that you feel is important to note in your journal so you can look back at it in the future.

Bonus Tips for Beginners

Make Sure You Have a Budget

Before you start to get too far into your day trading career, one of the first things you will want to do is sit down and work out your budget. I have discussed the types of bills you will have as a day trader and these are important to write in your budget. However, you also need to make sure that you know your starting budget for trading. You need to make sure that you have enough funds in order to start your day trading career. You will need to keep in mind the $25,000 minimum amount, but if you can't quite swing that, it doesn't mean that you can't start your trading career. You will just have to find a broker who will work with a trader who doesn't have the $25,000 minimum amount for an account.

You will also want to make sure that you keep up on your budget. Just because you get a start and you feel that you can make all your bills and continue to build up the amount in your trading account, doesn't mean you can stop paying attention to your budget. You want to sit down and take care of your budget every month.

You Don't Have to Trade Every Day

Even though it is important to keep up on your schedule and day traders often feel that they should work Monday through Friday, it is not necessary. This is something that you might feel you need to do in order to be able to live comfortably in your new career, however you also need to make sure that you can mentally handle your workload. If you have a really successfully day, you should look to see if you can take the next day off and give yourself a break if you need it. You want to remember to watch your mental health as well as your physical and emotional health because you need to have the right attitude if you want to become a successful day trader.

For some people, this involves trying to find a good work and life balance. This involves trying to get both their professional and home life connected over finding a balance so they can successfully handle both parts of their life.

Don't regret any day that you decide to take off. Even if you realize the next day that the market had a great day, it doesn't mean that you would have made a significant amount of money or that you missed out. Unfortunately, there are great stocks that day traders miss on a daily basis. It's all part of the job and one where you have to learn to move on, as it is in the past and no longer matters.

You Need to be Flexible

Some beginner day traders feel that they have to follow every rule exactly as it is stated and there is no room for flexibility. This is not true. In fact, you will start to find that you become more flexible the more you learn and the more you trade. This doesn't mean that you should ever completely ignore any rules, whether they were learned from your mentors, other day traders, or simply through your own research. You will still want to keep the rules in your mind but you will also want to make sure that you are fine with being flexible with these rules. There is always room for flexibility.

When you reach a healthy level of flexibility with your day trading career, you have realized that not everything is under your control. The flexibility will help you realize what you can control and what you cannot. It will help you realize that when you can't control what is in your environment, you focus on the factors that you can control and accept the rest.

You Can Access Different Devices

While I often talk about how you need to use your computer when you are working, you can use other devices to stay on top of market trends. This can help you stay mobile as you go about your day. For example, you can set up your account on your tablet or your phone. While you might not feel comfortable working directly from these devices for a long period of time, they will allow you to be able to check on a few things or complete certain tasks. However, you want to watch how much you do this, especially if you want to keep your work and personal life separate as much as possible. If you get into the habit of working on your phone or tablet while you are out with your family, you will start to lose your balance which can cause issues with both work life and personal life.

Chapter 6: Right Mental Mindset

to Have

Positivity is going to be the focus on the right mindset when it comes to day trading. While it is normal to feel a little anxious when you first start out, especially when you are making your first trade, you don't want this to affect your mindset. If you aren't positive about your day trading career, then you are less likely to succeed. In other words, you want to have what many day traders call a winning mindset.

Key Characteristics of the Winning Mindset

There are many key characteristics that you should have which will help you develop a winning mindset.

Realizing You Will Lose Sometimes

Many beginners have the idea that if they learn as much as they can about the market, they will be able to win every single trade they take on. However, this is not a characteristic of having a winning mindset. Instead, this is a characteristic that can make you disappointed in becoming a day trader and make you believe that this career isn't for you due to the lack of experiencing instasuccess. It can make you feel like a failure, which will give you the opposite mindset you need in order to become a successful day trader.

Be Your Own Type of Trader

It is easy to follow the ways of another trader, especially when you get advice from them. However, this won't allow you to become the most successful trader that *you* can be. Even as you listen to all the advice and help you will receive from other traders in your online communities or courses, you still need to remember to find your own system. You have to pick a technique that works for you. You need to be able to understand the strategy and you have to pick that trades you want to take part in.

In order to get into the right mindset as a trader, you have to always do your own research, always make sure that you understand everything in your business, and always make your own decisions. While you can get advice, no one should be doing these things for you, as then you are not reaching *your own* full potential.

Always be Confident in Your Abilities

Even when you are starting out as a day trader, you want to be confident in your abilities. Confidence will help you reap several benefits from within your mindset that will help you make decisions and move from any mistakes you make along your day trading journey. Another benefit of confidence is that it can help you move on from any bad trades.

Many people believe that the key to success is having confidence in your abilities. This is because of the benefits that people feel when they are confident in their careers. Some of these benefits are:

1. Increases Your Happiness

Above all, you will feel happier, not only in your job but in your life in general. When you feel happy with your life, you're going to feel better about what the tasks you have to accomplish. You will have more energy, feel more determined, and have the belief that you can take on the world if you work hard enough. At the same time, you will be able to help boost the happiness of the people around you, which includes any of your family members or people you converse with in your online forums.

2. Increases Your Health

Not only will you feel healthier because you feel better about yourself, but your mental health is also affected. When you feel positively about yourself, you aren't easily harmed by the challenges you face in life. You are able to move on from them more readily. On top of this, you are confident in being yourself, which will allow you to find the trader in you instead of following in the exact footsteps of your mentor or another experienced trader.

3. Increased Performance at Work

Because you feel more positive about yourself, you will be able to complete your daily tasks in a timely manner. You will feel that you can figure out any obstacles, and you know that you will give out the best work you possibly can because you are confident in your abilities. When you have stable self-confidence, you are going to be more successful because your overall work performance is going to increase.

4. You Won't Let Stress Get to You

People often start to feel stressed for a variety of reasons throughout their lives. This can often happen at work, especially as a day trader, as trading is a very high-pressure business. There are a lot of details you have to look over constantly, which can cause a lot of stress for people. However, the more confident you are in yourself, the less stress you will feel because you know that if you do your best you can accomplish the task.

You Are Consistent

Consistency is also a part of your winning mindset as a day trader. Not only will consistency help you improve yourself--especially when you are first starting out and more capable of making mistakes--but it will also help you understand who you are as a trader. You will start to learn what is most likely to happen when you remain consistent in your work day from your schedule to the strategy you use as a day trader. In fact, the more consistent you are in your job, the more successful you will find yourself.

You Have Self-Discipline

It is important to note that having self-discipline is a key characteristics of a day trader's winning mindset. This is because with self-control, day traders are able to focus on the important aspects of their job. They won't make hasty, rash decisions, they won't let too many distractions in and they understand there are situations they cannot control.

You Keep Your Emotions in Check

Any experienced trader will tell you that you always have to keep your emotions out of the business. At the same time, they will also tell you how hard this is. There are various techniques, from self-control to learning to remain calm, that will help you learn how to control your emotions. When you allow your emotions take over, you will start to make decisions based on those emotions. This will cause you to make the wrong decisions which can lead you to loss. On top of this, when you become emotionally invested in the market, you will start to lose interest as it starts to become less fun and more like something you have to do that causes you too much stress. A day trader who has a winning mindset will be able to keep their emotions in check most of the time. Furthermore, they will be able realize when his or her emotions are starting to take over. When this happens, it is best to take a break or back out of trading for the day.

Developing the Winning Mindset

There are many factors which go into helping you develop the winning mindset. Of course, some of these will be easier to develop than others. There will be some that will take you months, if not years, to get to the highest point possible. The key is to remember that you have to go at your own pace when you are developing your winning mindset. Just like you won't become a successful day trader overnight, you won't be able to reach your stable winning mindset overnight, especially if you struggle with self-control and self-confidence. However, this does not mean that you won't be able to become a successful day trader. You will just need to work on developing your winning mindset while you are also developing your skills as a day trader.

Make Sure You Stick to Your Daily Routine

Sticking to your routine is an essential part of developing your winning mindset. One reason for this is that your daily routine gives you a sense of structure. When you feel like you have structure, you are less likely to feel stressed. Instead, you are going to feel happy and start to gain self-confidence in your abilities. This means that if you lack self-confidence, sticking to your daily routine can help you increase this factor.

Successful day traders will tell you that they spend a lot of time making sure that their work day was well structured. Of course, many focused on structure for various reasons. Perhaps it helped them decrease stress, or perhaps it helped them feel like they would be more successful. Furthermore, making sure you follow your routine will help you keep up with your helpful habits.

Keep Yourself Accountable

As a day trader, you are your own boss. While some people handle this well, others may find that they struggle to make themselves accountable, which can lead to slacking in your trading responsibilities. Of course, this will only make you struggle more with your trading career. Therefore, one of the best ways to help you develop a winning mindset as your own supervisor is by making yourself accountable for every aspect within your job. Here are a few ways you can hold yourself accountable:

1. You want to set real goals for your trading career.

Before you even begin trading, you want to set real goals you can work towards accomplishing as a day trader. In fact, if you have not done this already, now would be the perfect time. You can start by thinking of the big goals you want to accomplish. Then you can create steps for each of these big goals. This way, you can work on the steps one by one and you won't start to feel overwhelmed by your own goals.

2. Start a trading journal and write in it every day.

We discuss how to keep a trading journal in greater depth in another chapter. Making sure you write in your trading journal is another great way you can hold yourself accountable in your job.

3. Make sure to review your trading plan often.

Your trading plan is an important part of starting your day trading business. This is the plan you will develop while you are working on starting up your new career. In fact, if you haven't started working on your trading plan, now would be the perfect time to start looking into creating this plan.

If you haven't developed your trading plan yet, here are a few steps to help you get started:

- Prepare yourself mentally. This is something you will want to make sure you do every day. If you find yourself feeling like you can't handle the stress of the stock market one day, then it would probably be in your best interest to take a break from trading. You will want to write down what you will do when this happens in your trading plan. Will you decide to calm your mind with meditation or other stress relievers and then see if you can take on the world of trading? Will you work on a relaxing hobby, so you can be better prepared to take on trading the next day? Whatever you feel you should do in order to help you prepare mentally for trading needs to be written down in your plan.

- Set your risk level. There is at least a little risk with every trade you will become a part of. Therefore, it is essential that you write down your risk level in your trading plan. You have to write down a level that you are comfortable with. Remember, you can always increase your risk level as you start to get more experience in the business. You also want to make sure to stick to this risk level, until you actively decide to make those changes.

- Make sure you create exit rules. You are going to find yourself in bad trades more often than you probably want to. While this does not mean that you are a bad trader, it does mean that you should have an exit plan for when you find yourself in this position.

- Make sure you create entry rules. Just as you create exit rules, you also want to make sure that you create entry rules that you will follow. These rules can discuss why and when you would buy a stock. They can also include several conditions that can help you figure out if you should take part in a trade or not.

Make Sure You Keep a Positive State of Mind

You not only want to keep a positive state of mind while you are in front of your computer and reports but also throughout your day in general. In fact, you want to do your best to make sure that you keep this frame of mind whether you are working or not. The more you keep this mindset, the easier it will be to maintain the mindset when you start to feel stressed or you find yourself in a bad trade.

Other than maintaining self-confidence and self-control, you also want to make sure you think counter-intuitively. The main aspect of this type of thinking is that you don't follow the thought process of other traders. This is another way that you will become your own trader and not someone who is just blindly following the herd. An example of this is when traders believe they see a breakout about to happen in one of their stocks, so they quickly make the next move to sell. However, the majority of the time, this ends up being a false breakout. When you think counter-intuitively, you aren't going to sell because you feel like this breakout isn't the real breakout.

This doesn't mean that you will spend your days getting the right breakout if you start to think counter-intuitively. In reality, it just means that no matter what is placed on your screen and what you have to deal with, you're not necessarily going to follow what the majority of other traders do at that moment, you are going to think for yourself and decide when the best time for you to trade is. Thinking this way will not always decrease your chances of losing, but it might help.

You Need to Truly Believe in Yourself

For many traders, truly believing in yourself is one of the hardest parts of developing the winning mindset. However, it is essential if you want to reach this attitude. This means that you not only have to believe in your abilities, but you also have to believe in your strengths, your self-control, your self-confidence, and in your success. Many people, especially if they struggle with any of these characteristics, are going to struggle to believe in themselves. However, it is essential, and as long as you continue to work towards believing, you will reach this state of mind.

If you struggle to believe in yourself, you first want to realize one fact: you are not alone. There are many people who find it difficult to believe in their abilities. There are also many people who take time out of their day to help build their belief system. If you know you have to start building up your belief system, so you can reach this feature, there are several books available to help you. However, to give you head start so you can get on the road to reaching the winning mindset, here are a few techniques to help you construct and scaffold your belief system.

1. Get rid of the words "impossible," "can't," and "never."

Our state of mind is heavily affected by the words we speak to ourselves. For example, if you are researching about day trading and start to doubt yourself, you might say, "I can never be successful at this." This sentence can affect your mindset more than you realize. When you feel yourself to start to use these words, you will want to focus on changing the negative words and sentences into positives. For instance, you could change the above sentence to, "I *will* be successful in day trading."

2. Surround yourself with positive, like-minded people. This is one reason it is important to become a member

of an online trading community, they are like-minded people who share the same interests. Furthermore, many of the people on the online forums have gone through the same processes you are, including developing the winning mindset. When you surround yourself with people who believe in themselves, they will give *you* the ability to believe in *yourself*.

3. Talk to people who have accomplished getting into and maintaining the winning mindset. It always helps when you get to know someone who has gone down the same path you are currently traveling down. When you join an online trading community and are struggling with your mindset, let other traders on the forum know this. There will be several traders who will come forward to help you reach your goals.

Chapter 7: Trading Strategies and Techniques

When it comes to trading, there are more strategies available than I can possibly put in one book. Part of the reason for this is because so many strategies can be used for different types of trading and investing. Another reason is that traders seem to be coming up with new forms of techniques all the time. However, I have chosen some of the most popular strategies that are used by day traders to outline here.

ABCD Pattern

This is a strategy that uses a specific pattern in order to help you find the exact time you should sell your stock. There are four parts to this pattern:

- A – the initial high price of the stock.

- B – the lowest price of the stock, which occurs when people start selling once they see the stock has hit A.

- C – the establishment of the higher low. This is the point where people who follow the ABCD pattern will start the selling process of their stock.

- D – the highest profitable point. This is the point the stock rises to, which gives the day trader a large profit.

This strategy is known to not only be a bit tricky, but also risky. This is because the trader has to sell at the specified point of C, which is when the stock starts to rise in price after reaching point B. Of course, the biggest risk is that the stock falls below point B *after* the trader sells at point C. This would mean that the trader receives a bigger loss than anyone who sold right after point A. However, the hope is that the price of the stock rises past point A, which gives the trader a large profit.

The ABCD pattern I explained above is just one of the patterns that you will see as a trader. Some patterns show point A to be the lowest price and point B to be the stock's highest price. However, the trader still sells at point C and hopes to reach point D to gain the best profit.

Bull Flag Momentum

This strategy received its bull flag name because the trend lines resemble a flagpole. After the stock reaches a high price, it has a short-term down trend. However, it quickly spikes up before spiking back down another time. This trend repeats one more time and leaves a pattern where the high prices and the low prices are parallel to each other. However, the pattern ends when the price spikes back up, exceeding the previous highest price. This is when traders begin to sell in hopes of making the best profit.

The trick to catching the bull flag strategy is that you look for the pattern where the high and low prices are parallel to each other, yet they are either slowly moving up or down the chart. Both of these directions signal that the stock can quickly spike up in price and exceed its previous high price.

Volume Weighted Average Price (VWAP) Trading

VWAP trading takes the price and volume of a stock to give you an average price. It is known as a trading benchmark, and will give traders an idea of the trend and security of the stock. Like most trading strategies, the VWAP can be used with specific software that will perform the algorithms for each step. However, it is possible to calculate the VWAP yourself.

This type of strategy can be used by various investors and traders. For example, both day traders and buy-and-hold investors can use the VWAP technique. However, it is more popular with short-term trades. This strategy will start new at the beginning of the day and give you a running total at the end of the day. This is one of the reasons buy-and-hold investors use this strategy, as it allows them to analyze the stock.

Electronic Communication Network (ECN) and Level II

This type of strategy involves watching the trades in real time. It is similar to going to a horse race and watching the race to see if you are going to win or lose your money. The ECN is an automated system where traders from all over can trade with you. Day traders who take on the business by themselves, without the help of a broker, usually use the ECN strategy because it's fairly easy to navigate and is known to take out any middleman. This is a benefit as it takes away any brokerage fees and can make trades more profitable because it is known to save time. On top of this, the ECN allows for after-market trading, which means you can trade after the regular trading hours of the day.

There are several charts available that will allow you to see the price changes of stocks throughout the day. All of the charts will allow you to compare the opening price to the closing price. On top of this, the charts will also allow you to see the various price changes in the stock during the day.

1. Candlestick Charts

Most day traders use candlestick charts as they find them essential for the business. These charts are helpful because they will display specific security prices on a daily basis. Once you learn how to analyze candlestick charts, you will be able to tell when the highest and lowest prices for any of your stocks will be, which will help you increase your profits. Furthermore, you will be able to learn where the stock sits at both opening and closing that day. If the candlestick has a red or black color, then the closing price of the stock is lower than the opening price. If the candlestick has a green or white color, then you know that the closing price is higher than the opening price. You can also analyze more about the stock through the shadow of the candlestick. The shadow will tell you what the prices were throughout the stock's day. You can then take this analysis and compare it to the opening and closing prices.

2. Line Charts

Line charts are another popular chart type that day traders use often. While these charts give you the same information as candlestick charts, they will only work if you have the specified charting software. However, this is becoming more typical with any type of chart you want to use. This is because the charting software that is on the market today will allow you to develop the charts you want to use and include all the information you need in order to analyze the stocks on a daily basis.

3. Bar Charts

Many day traders like to use bar charts because they are some of the easiest charts to read. There are four main prices that you will find if you use bar charts. The first one is the opening price. The second price is the highest price and the third is the lowest price of the day. The final price you will see through the chart is the closing price. Through these four prices, you can start to analyze what the day-to-day process is for any stock you are interested in.

Spread Trading

Spread trading, also known as scalping, is defined as trading securities over a period of seconds to minutes. The reason this type of technique has become popular is because traders feel that they can catch stocks easier when they follow small growths over large increments. The number of transactions day traders go through can vary from a dozen to over 200 within a day. Traders make so many transactions because they will sell the stock as soon as it will give them a profit.

This type of technique is known to be relatively safe, which is another reason why so many traders consider themselves spread traders. Traders who follow this technique are often considered to be market makers, as they help maintain the liquidity of the market.

If you are thinking about looking more into this strategy, then you will want to note the following three points:

Low Profits Comes from Large Volume

Traders who use the spread trading technique state this strategy is not useful for people who want to move large volumes of shares at one time. They will not be able to make the money they want by using this strategy as large volumes give low profits. This happens because the profit margin, which is the measure of profitability, neglects the large volume investor. Therefore, the best type of traders for spread trading are the ones who are interested in moving small volumes.

You Will Have a Lower Risk if You Lower Your Exposure

Traders who take on the technique of scalping will limit their risk of loss because they don't hang onto their stocks for a long period of time. In fact, most traders will hold on to the majority of their shares for only a few minutes, very rarely reaching an hour.

Smaller Moves are Easier

I have already stated that you want to move small volumes in order to gain the best benefits as a spread trader. People who follow this technique become pros at finding the small moves with the small spreads that tend to happen frequently throughout the day. The reason spread traders focus on small moves is not only because they are easier to handle using this technique but also because this is where they will find their best profits.

Trend Following

Traders refer to trend following as trading stocks because of their trends over their market value. This type of technique is not only used in day trading, but in all types of stock market transactions. How long you will follow the trend before you decide to take a stock because of its trend depends on what type of trading you are doing. In day trading, you won't spend more than a couple of hours on the trend. However, if you are into swing trading, you might analyze the trend for a few days to a couple of weeks.

Many traders like to take part in this technique because they feel that they know what the stock is going to do. Because you have watched for a trend to develop and then analyzed the trend to make sure it's a purchase you would like to make, your confidence about what the stock will do in the future increases. On top of this, many traders feel that they are more likely to succeed in making a profit because they can watch for stocks that will give you capital instead of loss.

At the same time, you always want to pay attention to all the factors that affect the trend of a stock. The factors you should consider if you decide to use trend following are:

Money Management

Money management is one consideration, as if you have too much money, then you are at a risk of losing more money than you should. However, if you don't have enough money, you are unlikely to reap the benefits of that trade. When you look at money management, you pay a lot of attention to your risk, which will let you know how much money you should put into that stock.

Price

The most important factor you will want to pay attention to is the price of the stock. While day traders pay attention to price variations of the stock, the most important price to look at is the actual price of the stock in the moment. It is the actual price that will tell you whether you should invest in the stock or hold off.

Diversity

Diversity is a word that you will often see in the stock market. This refers to the different types of stocks that you have in your portfolio. This is also a term that you will find some traders following while some traders feel it's a waste of time. While it is controversial, there are many benefits of diversity, especially for traders and serious investors. On top of this, when you use diversity, you are able to follow trends better, as it is an important factor of trend following.

Risk

Another factor to consider is the amount of risk that comes with the trend. While you can never get rid of *all* the risk in trading, you want to limit it as much as possible. If you find you are looking at a trend that is high in risk, you may want to pick a different stock, especially as a day trader. However, there are traders who like stocks with higher risk. How much risk you are willing to take on in a stock is a personal preference. However, most experienced day traders say that if you truly want to be successful, you will limit your risk as much as possible.

Rules

Finally, you will always want to follow the rules. Not only follow the rules of day trading, but you will also want to follow the rules you have created for yourself. One reason for this is it helps you remain consistent in your trading, which will help increase your success rate. Another reason is because your rules will help you become systematic when you are choosing your stocks.

News Playing

This is a technique day traders use when they follow the news of the stock market. When most people think of the stock market, they imagine a person reading the newspaper to see how the price of stocks is doing that day. This is similar to news playing, however, most day traders pay attention to several sources of information. You can get the news information from any online communities you join, news outlets, or any other reports which are easily found online.

One of the most important factors when following the news playing technique is to make sure you keep your emotions in check. Experienced traders know well how emotions can affect your decisions when trading. They also know how this can cause a trader to lose a lot of money. One of the most popular historic examples of how emotions can affect the stock market is the stock market crash of 1929. This is the event that helped launch the United States into the Great Depression, which lasted throughout the 1930s. One of the reasons the crash occurred was because of all the investors who decided to quickly sell their stocks because they saw prices dropping. They started to get anxious over the money they would lose if they didn't sell. On top of that, they started to worry about the stock market in general because the prices were becoming so low. Emotions were running high on Wall Street right before the stock market crash, which did not help the situation at all. In fact, many historians state that if people would have kept their stocks instead of selling them, America would have never seen such a horrible depression in its economy. As stated before, when stocks sell, the price declines. Therefore, the more people who sell, the more the price will drop. Because the price of stocks kept dropping, more people started to sell. Eventually, this led to the stock market crash.

It is always a good thing to make sure you are thinking logically when you are making decisions in the stock market. If you find yourself thinking illogically, you are putting too much emotion into your decision. One of the best things to do when this happens is simply to take a break or pick a stock that you don't feel too much emotion towards. It's also important to remember that day trading isn't for everyone. If you are naturally a person with strong emotions, you might want to look at different trading or investing methods.

You also want to make sure that you continue to do your research. Once you see a news report, you want to look into how this news is affecting the stock. For example, if you read that CVS Pharmacy donated thousands of dollars to a struggling community, you might find their stock prices increasing. The news can easily affect who buys and sells a company's stocks, as investors want to purchase stocks from companies they believe will be successful and are proud to own a share of. Therefore, the price of the stock will go up, but the value might also increase.

Of course, there is always negative news which can also affect stocks. If you find that you hold a stock in a company and you see a negative news article about them, you will probably want to sell your stock as quickly as possible because this will allow you to sell with less loss.

Fading

Not a lot of traders take part in fading because it is known to be one of the riskier strategies. Unless you have a good amount of experience in trading, it is best that you don't participate in fading, as it is considered a more advanced technique in the business. The basis of short selling is that the trader speculates on the stock's decline. Speculation means that the trader makes the transaction when the risk of losing capital is high because the trader expects that there will be a benefit or some type of gain from the trade.

Fading doesn't follow the trends of the market. They buy when the price of the stock is low and sell when the price is high. They often buy a stock when they feel the market has overreacted over recent news. One of the benefits is that there is little analysis that needs to be done before buying or selling.

Stop-Loss Trading

This type of strategy involves making a deal with your broker to sell a stock once it reaches a certain price. This is a popular strategy, in fact most experienced traders say you should use stop-loss trading because it gives you security in your business. This happens because you can decide to say that you will sell the stock when it is 13% below your purchasing price.

This type of strategy isn't always used to for day trading because sometimes the stock won't reach the percentage you set. Therefore, you continue to hold the stock and don't sell it at the end of the day.

Range Trading

Range trading is often compared to trend following, however they are different techniques. When you use range trading, you will watch a stock over a certain period of time. Like other techniques, the increase and decline of prices will present a pattern which is noticeable to the trader. The trader will watch the prices until they see a breakout in the pattern. A breakout is when the price dramatically inflates. The opposite of this, a breakdown, is when the price dramatically declines from its pattern. Once this happens, traders feel that this pattern will continue for some time.

In order to reduce risks when it comes to this strategy, traders will often set high and low limits. This means that once they have viewed where the stock's pattern is sitting for a couple of hours, they will set the highest and lowest price they will buy or sell. Then, once the breakout or breakdown occurs, the trader will take the step and buy or sell the stock.

Chapter 8: Trading Strategies for Various Financial Instruments

Stocks

Stocks are typically one of the first things people think of when they look into trading. When it comes to the stock market, people usually refer to stocks as shares. There are many ways you can go about handling shares. For example, if you are interested in investing, you might use the buy and hold strategy, which is when you buy stocks and keep them for as long as you want. Usually, people try to keep them over the long term.

However, when you are looking into day trading, you will handle shares differently as you don't want to hold on to them for a long time. When you are looking to purchase stocks, you will want to find those shares that are working their way up or already at the bottom on their fall. By doing this, you should be able to make some type of profit by the end of the day.

When reading about the stock market, many people will tell you not to pay attention to the stock prices throughout the day, as they normally jump up and down. While you will want to take this advice if you are investing in the stock market, you do not want to follow this advice if you are a day trader. In fact, as a day trader you want to make sure that you are paying close attention to the prices of stocks for your target companies every day. You want to watch how much they fall and rise because this will let you know if you should take one of the company's shares or not.

The best shares for you to purchase in the morning are the ones that are facing a decline because of an unforeseen event. This can be any type of event, including negative news or investors feeling that the price is declining too rapidly and, therefore, decide to sell their shares. One of the main reasons why prices rise and decline is because people are buying or selling the stocks. For example, if a large number of people buy shares from Target, the price is going to rise. However, if they decide to sell their shares, the price is going to decline. Typically, especially for a strong business like Target, any decline is temporary and the price soon rises again. This is one reason is it important that you keep up to date on the stock market.

Currencies

When you decide to take currencies on in your day trading career, you will find your risk increasing because you become both the buyer and the seller. While this always increases any risk in your trading, it is best to have a little experience before you start trading in currencies. However, if you have ever traveled to another country where you had to exchange your funds you will understand how trading currencies works as it is similar. For example, if you are traveling from Canada to the United States, you will have to exchange your Canadian money for United States money. The same goes for trading as a day trader. You will be able to trade your currency for any currency around the world, but you will want to make sure you are well versed in the currency so you can receive the best capital gain.

ETFs

ETFs (exchange traded funds) are collections of stocks, commodities, or other investment types. Basically, it is a basket of assets that you can purchase without having to buy each individual stock. One ETF can own hundreds of stocks from various companies. Traders can buy and sell ETFs just as they would individual stocks throughout the day. When an ETF is purchased, shareholders do not own the underlying asset--instead, they own a share or a portion of each stock within the basket.

Futures

Dealing in futures is not only known as the best option for day traders, but it's also the best place for a beginner to start their career. When you think of futures, you can think of a contract. This contract is between two people who state that one part will sell shares at a specific time in the future. The timing of this sale typically depends on the on the price of the stock, and within the agreement both parties will settle on a price.

Futures can also help decrease risk, as you are able to watch for a price in which you will make a good profit. Another benefit of using futures is that they allow for beginners to learn more about the stock market through hands-on experience. While you always want to make sure you are educated before you start, you also want to continue your education after you have begun. Through futures, a person is able to get a better picture of how the stock market works and how to look into where stocks are heading in the future.

Options

When it comes to stock options, the trader has the right to an agreed-upon price for a stock. At the same time, the trader can select a specific date when buying and selling, according to the agreement. There are two different types of options. The first is known as calls and the second type is called puts. The calls give you the right to buy the stock following the agreement, and the puts give you the right to sell.

This is known to be a benefit to anyone who is trading in the stock market because of the flexibility within the trade. For example, you can purchase the stock option when it is low but you don't have to quickly sell it. Instead, you can wait for the price to increase, which is when you complete the purchase and sell the share. This helps in making sure that you are able to gain a profit. Day traders like to use stock options because it help decrease their risk of losing capital.

Forex

Forex is the shortened term for the Foreign Exchange Market, which is where you would trade your currencies. Currently, this is one of the most heavily used markets online because everyone from companies to individual traders is utilizing it. In fact, you don't have to be a day trader to participate in Forex trading, as you will use this market whenever you may travel around the world and need to exchange currency.

Like any other form of trading, there are a few things you need to know before you start trading currency.

- Each currency is designated by its own symbol in the market. For example, the United States dollar is USD.

- There is a market price associated with each Forex pair. The price tells you how much of the second currency you will need to trade for the first currency.

- Currencies are always traded in pairs. No matter what transaction you are making, you have to trade one currency with another.

- You don't have to have a certain amount of money in your account to start Forex trading as there is no minimum requirement.

- You can trade currencies in through three different units: mini, micro, and standard lots.

- When you first start Forex trading, experts suggest that you start with the micro account, which is $1,000, as this allows for more flexibility.

Chapter 9: Fundamental Analysis

Most recently, fundamental analysis has seen its share of controversy in the day trading world. While some traders feel that this type of analysis has no place in day trading, other people state that without it, traders would not be able to complete their trades successfully. In a nutshell, when it comes to fundamental analysis, it might come down to personal preference more than anything else. Again, it is important that you become your own individual trader. This means that it is 100% up to you to decide if you will used fundamental analysis in your career or not.

How fundamental analysis works is by trying to analyze the future of a stock by providing data which focuses on the whole of the economy's underlying forces. However, analyzing the economy as a whole is just part of fundamental analysis. Other factors include analyzing a stock's company and the true value of the stock.

There are two main types of fundamental analysis. The first type in known as bottom-up and the second type is known as top-down. When you focus on the second type, you will first look at the global and national economic factors and then look at your stock to see how the factors will affect your security. When you focus on the bottom-up type, you basically flip the scenario around: instead of looking at the economic factors first, you look at the security, which will help you decide when the best time to sell the stock will be.

Another way to look at fundamental analysis is by stating that more experienced traders profit from beginners or traders with less skill than they have. However, this isn't to say that fundamental analysis is a low business with experienced people profiting from people new to the market. It is simply how the system works when looking at the whole of the trading economy.

In order to help you better understand how this works, there are three factors that go into fundamental analysis that show that more experienced traders can profit from less experienced people.

1. Companies that issue additional stock and initial public offerings are one means by which experienced traders can profit from others. Basically, the initial public offerings give you an opportunity to cash in on your stock's discrepancy. These often occur when stocks are sold or traded at a lower price than what the trader purchased them for. In a sense, this is a settled price which a less experienced trader can give a more experienced trader.

2. Another way experienced traders make money through the less experienced ones is because they tend

to be quicker. This doesn't mean that the more experienced trader is trying to scam others out of money. It simply means that he or she has more experience than someone else and, therefore, has a better sense of when to trade a stock. Day trading is a learning profession that takes years to fully gain the grasp of. Because of this, you will often feel that there are thousands of other traders who are taking advantage of an opportunity. In reality, they are not trying to take anything away from you, they are just quicker when it comes to trading. It's a stage you can reach, as well, if you continue to work hard and remain determined and positive.

3. Experienced traders tend to take more risk because they can handle the risk. This means that they will often focus on more established companies and be able to find the exact moment when they should trade in order to make a profit.

While fundamental analysis is still an important thing for many day traders, it is not as popular as technical analysis, which we will take a look at next.

Chapter 10: Technical Analysis

Technical analysis is the study of past marketing trends. This becomes important to day traders because past trends can often help you predict what could happen with the stock in the future. Of course, you will always want to remember that just because it happened in the past, does not mean that the pattern will continue in the future. However, the chances are still pretty high that the trend will continue. You just want to ensure that you don't have the attitude that it will be the exact same because, even if the pattern continues, there will always be some changes.

Of course, there is more that goes into technical analysis than what the past marketing trends show. Like anything else in your day trading career, you will want to make sure you are educated in technical analysis, so you know how to look at the various graphs that you will encounter along the way. On top of this, you will also want to use other techniques to help you get close to any future prediction. These other techniques you will learn throughout your research on the topic, but can include how to make general predictions and gathering your basic understanding of the stock market.

Technical analysis is popular among a lot of different investors and traders. However, not all day traders will find technical analysis to be a useful part of their system. It all depends on your personal preference when it comes to how you want to go about choosing your stocks.

What You Will Find through Technical Analysis

When you start to read the past marketing trends of stocks, you will find a variety of graphs and charts that you will use to conduct technical analysis. We touched on some of these earlier, such as candlestick charts, bar charts, and line charts, but there are several other charts that could be of use to you while you conduct your technical analysis.

Price Charts

The price chart is described as the center chart in technical analysis. In this chart, there are two separate lines. One is a vertical line that describes the price, and the horizontal line describes the time.

Point and Figure Chart

While this is the chart that has been around the longest--well over a century--it is also one you won't find very often anymore. However, this doesn't mean that it is less important than any of the other charts you can find when looking at a stock's history. While this chart won't indicate volume or time, it can be an excellent chart that will help you predict where the price of the stock is going to go in the future.

One thing that sets the point and figure chart apart from the rest is that instead of being made up of points and lines, it is made up of x's and o's, which can make it easier to read for some people. When you see an "o" on the chart, this means that the price decreased. When you see an "x" on the chart, it means that the price increased.

People who find the point and figure chart useful will often take a quick glance at the chart and as they can easily spot the x's and o's without having to do a close analysis. For some traders, this quick analysis will give them enough information on whether it is a stock they want to look into further or not. However, the best idea is always to continue your analysis, no matter how the chart looks to you at first glance. It is important to remember that whatever you are doing in the world of trading, you want to be as thorough as you possibly can. If you don't take your time, you can easily miss something of importance that could have given you a sizable profit--or protected you from sizable loss--if you'd only taken it into consideration.

No matter what chart you decide to use when you are conducting technical analysis, you will find the different prices within that chart. These prices will be some of the most important features of your analysis. Through these charts, you will be able to find out what the price of the stock was when it opened, when it closed, what its peak price was, and what its lowest price was.

Range or Trend

Once you come across a chart you are going to analyze, you will want to think about where your interest is, whether it is with the range of the trend of the stock. Even though the range and the trend are different, they both have to do with the price which is why they are important for you to look at when it comes to technical analysis.

If you decide that trend is more appealing to follow, then you are more interested in going with the flow. Furthermore, you are probably more comfortable with risk than someone who would pick to follow the range. You will often find out what other people are doing while you look at the trend. While this isn't something that you should get into the habit of as a trader because following others can make you lose sight of your individual trading habits, it is important to follow if this is what is more appealing to you during your analysis. However, the trend is also considered to be the riskier choice of the two.

The reason following the trend is riskier is not because you are going with what other people are doing but because you are using the trend and trying figure out the best future prediction you can on where the stock is going. Because of the risk, you will want to make sure that you keep your trades small. Remember, the larger your trades are, the riskier they become. Even if you are comfortable with a large level of risk, you don't want to take on *too* much risk on the same stock.

If you decide that range is more important, then you probably have a lower level of risk that you are comfortable taking on as a trader. There is nothing wrong with having a lower level of risk, in fact, as a beginner it can help you in the long run. On top of this, you can always build up to techniques and stocks that carry more risk as you continue to learn more about the world of day trading.

The reason why range is generally safer is because it allows you to predict where the price of the stock is going to move in the future with more confidence. You are able to take your education, your analysis, and all the other factors and combine them to give you a more reliable future prediction with the stock.

When you focus on the range, you are looking to see when the stock is going to move positively, which is when you will make your move and take on the stock. This positive movement will often come before the price declines again, which means that you usually have a very short window to trade this stock, if you decide to take it on. This doesn't mean that you have to find the best point of entry, it simply means that you want to be aware when you believe the time will be and then make yourself available for a possible entry. If you find that you missed your opportunity when you go back to the stock, don't dwell on that. Remember, it is impossible to predict the future of a stock 100%, no matter how well you conducted your analysis.

Technical Analysis and Psychology

If you have any background in psychology, you are going to find technical analysis pretty easy to understand. In fact, you will probably grow to love technical analysis and use it as often as possible. There is a lot of psychology that goes into this because you are essentially analyzing the behavioral patterns of the stocks and traders who took part in creating those patterns.

In fact, psychology can help you in blocking off one of the biggest risk factors when it comes to using technical analysis: getting your emotions tied up in your decisions. As I have discussed before, you want to make sure that you keep your emotions out of your decisions when it comes to trading. Psychology can help you curb your emotions when you are analyzing the stock's behavior because you are more likely to become aware of your emotions when it comes to technical analysis.

One of the biggest emotions you want to make sure you are aware of is greed. This emotion can quickly pop up without people realizing it, especially when their trades are going great and they find themselves making a good amount of money. It is a natural human reaction to feel that once you start profiting from your job, you want to find ways to make more money. In return, you can start to get a sense of greed when you are looking for your next profit, which can cause all kinds of problems and mistakes along the way that could last well into your future.

Another way psychology and technical analysis go together is because of the self-fulfilling prophecy. Because so many other traders have used the same system, you come to realize that the strategies they use do work. This can help you in many ways, including boosting your confidence when making decisions.

Chapter 11: Managing Risk

No matter what type of trading you decide to take on, or even if you decide to take the investing route later, you will have to manage your risk. Fortunately, there are a lot of tips from experienced day traders that will help you with risk management Unfortunately, there is no way to get rid of risk completely. Like with any other career, there is always a chance for something to go differently than we expected it to.

Strategies to Help You Manage Risk

The 1% Risk Rule

One of the most popular strategies day traders use to manage risk is known as the 1% risk rule. This rule is pretty basic and states that you never risk more than 1% of your account value on any given trade. However, this doesn't mean that you can only take 1% of your capital to buy a trade. For example, if you only have $50,000 in your capital account, don't think you can only take $500 of that for any trade. The rule means that you focus on various risk management steps in order to help you prevent more than 1% of *loss* on a trade.

While the 1% rule is known to be the most popular risk management strategy, there is another one that is close behind and follows the same method. This rule is known as the 2% rule. Basically, instead of only investing 1% of your account value, you can invest up to 2% of your account value. In fact, many traders will start by following the 1% rule in the beginning but as they gain more experience and acquire more capital, they will start to use the 2% rule as a risk management strategy.

Don't Trade Alone

Another popular risk management strategy is to find a broker or an advisor who will help you through your trading process. I will again emphasize that not only should you feel like you can completely trust this person, but you also need to make sure that they have a great amount of trading experience. While investors can be helpful, you need to remember that investing and trading are separate. Therefore, you want to focus on finding someone who has been a trader, specifically a day trader, to help you learn the rules, guidelines, and other factors related to the world of trading.

While you can eventually start to trade alone, you want to make sure that you understand the day trade career and feel completely comfortable with working own your own. It might take a few years to reach this point, and that is completely fine. You want to remember that you are focusing on a new career, whether it is part-time or full-time. Therefore, you need to put the best you have into this career and if that means you have a broker or mentor for the first few years, then you handled your new job well.

It's Fine to Just Cut Your Losses

The stop-loss rule is one of the biggest ways that you can minimize your risk. This rule should be a part of your trading plan and will tell you exactly when you need to trade or sell your stock no matter how much money you will lose. Basically, this gives you a limit to how much you are allowed to see the price drop before you have to make the move to cut your losses.

It is also important to remember at this time that you should not take any of your losses to heart. If you want to become a successful day trader, you will need to understand that sometimes you win and sometimes you lose. When you lose, it is important to just move on and focus on your next step.

Note Other Day Trader Mistakes

It cannot be emphasized enough: every day trader makes mistakes. Unfortunately, there is no way around this. However, you can limit the number of mistakes *you* make by knowing what common mistakes *others* make and avoiding following in their misplaced footsteps. Let's discuss a few of these.

You Find Yourself Trading Too Much

Trading too much can often become a problem when you have decided to make day trading your full-time job. There is a lot of information about day trading. No matter how much people try, to be able to fit all the information you have to know about day trading into one book is nearly impossible. This is why people often have a few books about day trading. For example, they might start with a beginner's guide and then move onto more advanced strategies and information.

Because of this, you might feel that you can become a full-time day trader but then quickly feel overwhelmed once you start officially trading. Sometimes people find that they aren't making the profits they need to right away, which is common, so they decide to take on more trades during the day. However, this is when they start making more mistakes. On top of this, people can find they are starting to lose interest in a career they were once excited about.

If you find yourself in this situation, don't think that you have made a mistake in becoming a full-time day trader. Instead, look at how often you are trading. You are likely trading too much, and you need to work on finding a more comfortable pace for yourself as a day trader. This could mean that as you are still learning the basics about day trading, decide to be a part-time trader before working your way up to being a full-time trader.

If you find yourself in this situation, don't spend too much time worrying about how you got there. Instead, work on how you can keep yourself from getting into this situation again. It can take some time, and it might mean that you need to focus on one stock at a time while finding your "groove." However, the outcomes of taking a step back and finding a more comfortable level for yourself will give you more benefits and higher profits than taking on too many of the wrong stocks at the wrong times.

You Have Unrealistic Expectations

When most people get into day trading, they know very little about it, and this can lead to unrealistic expectations. There is nothing wrong with finding out your expectations do not quite match up with reality when you get started in your new trading career. In fact, if you think about it, most people entering new positions will often have unrealistic expectations. It's all a part of the system, which is why this is one of the most common mistakes that beginners make as they enter the field.

While you might not be able to stop all of your unrealistic expectations, you can cut down on the amount by making sure you do all the research you possibly can before getting into day trading. On top of this, it is always a good idea to become a member of an online community where you can spend some time talking to other traders and getting an idea as to what is realistic and what isn't when it comes to your expectations.

One of the biggest unrealistic ideas that new day traders have is that they are missing a secret formula when it comes to choosing the best stocks. I can tell you right now, there is absolutely no secret formula when it comes to picking the best stocks that will give you the most profit. Therefore, you don't want to spend your time and energy looking for "the one," as all you will do is waste your energy and time. Instead, you want to spend your time researching information that will be helpful to a beginner.

Like any other mistake that is made in the day trading world, it is important not to let mistakes (and dwelling on them) take a lot of your time. If you find that you have unrealistic expectations, simply let them go and move on to the next step. Figure out what is more realistic and focus on the positives of your new career.

Not Following Through with Your Post-Trading Analysis

It is critical to take time every day to conduct post-trading analysis. In fact, this is just as important as making sure you take time in the morning for your pre-trading analysis. You have to make sure that your post-trading analysis is a part of your business plan. On top of this, you have to make sure that you take the time every day you trade to write in your trading journal, screenshot your trades, find any mistakes you made, look at the ways in which you performed well, and any other analyses that are important to you. If you don't follow through with this, you won't be able to grow as a day trader.

When you are analyzing your trades for the day, you want to remember the five "w"s, which are who, what, where, when, and why.

1. Who

When you are asking who made the trade, you should be able to point to yourself. However, if you find that you are thinking about other people, this means that you let others tell you to make this trade. Because it is important to keep in mind that *you* should be deciding what trades you make, if you find yourself pointing to others you have found a weakness that you need to work on.

2. What

The what part of your analysis will include any factors pertaining to the stock, such as what the price was, any stop-loss prices, profits, and strategies you used. One of the best ways to make sure you don't miss any detail of this section is to create a template that you can use every time you are going through a stock's post-trade analysis.

3. Where

This part of your post-trade analysis is pretty simple. It is basically making sure you note where you were when you decided to take on the trade. For example, were you sitting in your office or in your living room? Were you using your computer or a mobile device?

If you are wondering why this is important, think about how your lifestyle can affect your trading. If you are a stay-at-home parent who has decided to take on trading part-time to help earn a little extra income, then the where will tell you if distraction may have played a role when you made this trade. This can help you note settings in which you should or should not be making trades.

4. When

You could also benefit from using a template when you look at the when a trade was made. For this, you can not only write down the date of the trade but the time you made the trade. Furthermore, you can write down any other important information regarding dates or times, such as when you started focusing on this particular stock as a possible trade. How specific you are with this depends on your personal preference. You might find that you are not as specific as you should be after a few months, so you decide to include more detail after review.

5. Why

This is a part of your post-trade analysis that you might find yourself changing the most often, at least at the beginning of your career. This is the area that you might find to be one of the most important because it will give you as much detail as you want to record, from why you decided to take on the trade to why you decided to sell the stock when you did. This section can give you a lot of information about your overall trading personality that you didn't really catch on to before. On top of this, you might be able to find out what some of your strengths and weaknesses are through this practice.

Not Following Through with Your Pre-Trade Activities

This is one of the most common mistakes beginner day traders make. Your pre-trade analysis will often include seeing what the stock market did overnight, how the Forex market did, and reading up on the latest news. This part of the day should be completed before the stock market opens, which can be a bigger challenge for some people than others, depending on where a person lives and their time zone relative to the stock exchange.

Because you have to follow the New York Stock

Exchange time zone, if you live in California, this means that the market opens at about 6:30 in the morning. If you are more of a night owl than an early bird, this time can turn into a challenge for you. However, if you are determined to be a successful day trader, then you will be able to overcome this obstacle.

You should at least allow yourself a half hour to an hour before the stock market opens to go through your pre-trade activities. If you find that you need more or less time, you can always adjust as you start to get comfortable in your new profession.

Day traders who have made the mistake of not following through with their pre-trade analysis often note that they started to make more mistakes throughout their day. On top of this, they felt like they didn't truly understand what was going on with the stock they were looking at because they had not read the latest news, which can quickly affect the stocks for a company. Avoiding this mistake is easy, as all you have to do is make sure you have enough self-discipline to allow yourself enough time in the morning to conduct this analysis.

You Don't Worry About Your Mental Health

Not worrying enough about your mental health is a common mistake in nearly all professions, not just day trading. And just like other occupations, making sure you have the right state of mind is going to lead you toward or away from success. I'll say it again: when it comes to day trading, having the right mindset can determine if you are going to have a winning or losing attitude.

The key to not getting caught up in this mistake is simply to make sure you are not taking on too much at once. If you start feeling like you are taking on too many trades, you are working too long, or you are overstressed, your mental health is going to start to decline. One of the dangers of a decline in mental health is you don't often realize that it is on a downward spiral until you are completely exhausted or have lost all self-confidence.

In order to keep yourself from making this mistake, you need to remember a couple of main points. First, you need to have patience and you have to remember that patience is an important part of trading. Second, you need to continue to educate yourself, as this will help you learn a good balance in your career. Not only will your education help you in learning how day trading works and all the details that go into the profession, but it can also help you realize where *you* can comfortably sit as a day trader. Through your education, you might find that it is best to stick with three trades instead of four, or one trade instead of two. You can always work your way back up after you have established solid footing with regard to your mental health.

Believing That Anyone Can Become a Day Trader

Unfortunately, day trading isn't for everyone. One of the most common mistakes traders make is believing that *anyone* can do it. Part of this comes from the fact that people often feel that if they can accomplish some specific thing, then anyone can. This isn't true when it comes to day trading. For example, some people might be better suited for investing in the stock market, such as by using the buy and hold strategy. Other people might find that they like to keep their investments to bonds, CDs, or a high-interest savings account.

Of course, this doesn't mean that someone who isn't educated about day trading can't become a day trader. In reality, if someone is informed, determined, and willing to work hard towards their career, they can become a successful day trader. However, it is important to note that a person must have these traits or they could find themselves losing more capital than they ever imagined.

Chapter 12: What Does a Typical Trading Day Look Like?

One thing you should understand as a day trader is that timing is of critical importance. If you go back and look at the strategies and techniques you read earlier, you will notice that that when traders buy and sell, they do it at specific times. This can be more challenging with some strategies than others because, as the spread strategy shows, traders buy and sell constantly.

One of the ways you can understand timing and how a day trader's workday flows is by looking at a typical trader's schedule. Of course, your time zone will affect when you actually get up to start work. Because you work around the regular stock market hours, which are 9:30 am to 4 pm Eastern Time, you will need to adjust your hours. For example, if you live on the west coast, your day will start around 6:30 am. Because the time zone for the stock market is based on Eastern Time, the times listed below follow this time zone.

Before the Market Opens

Most traders begin their day before the market opens. This not only allows them to get ready for their job in terms of getting ready for the day (having coffee and grabbing something for breakfast), but it also allows them to catch up on the news and changes that occurred overnight in the stock market. In fact, many experienced day traders will tell you that the most important part of the day is the first half hour. This is the time when you will check on the stocks and look for ones that you might want to observe for a couple of hours or take on.

This is also the time of the day where the market is unstable. One of the reasons for this is the morning news. People are learning what has changed overnight and the stock market changes rapidly for about a half hour or so. Therefore, it is always best to *not* do any buying or selling during this time. In fact, most traders tend to sit on the sidelines and watch the market, as this can keep them from losing money.

It is at this moment that you will want to make sure that all your technology is up and running. You will want to make sure that your internet is not malfunctioning, that your computer has completed any updates and is ready to perform the day's tasks, and that your scanner, printer, and anything else is turned on and ready to go. It is always wise to open your trading platform and any other software tools that you will need to complete your tasks for the day at this time. Take the time to make sure that everything is running smoothly. If you notice any issues, you will want to make sure you do what you can to fix the issues so you can be prepared to take on the stock market world as soon as possible without having technical difficulties ruin your day.

The Morning Stock Market

After you have guaranteed that everything is working correctly and you are ready to face the day, you should start scanning the market. You will want to check out any stocks you had in mind to watch previously, and check to see which stocks you should keep an eye on or purchase. You will start to pay attention to the trends, notice any breakouts and breakdowns, and see what stocks are performing well and which ones aren't. During this time, at least from about 9:30 to 10:00 am, you will start to see which stocks could give you the best profits for the day.

Many experienced traders have said that around the 10:00 hour is when things will start to slow down. Of course, there will always be traders selling and buying throughout the day, but the volatile morning session is over and now traders are working towards figuring out their next steps.

Between 10:30 am and 11:00 am, many traders will cash out the trades they see as profitable. While some will quit for the day, others will continue their work in the stock market, especially if they haven't been able to make a profit yet. As you find the stock market calming down, you will notice a few who are working towards buying a new stock that they hope to be able to sell at the end of the day for a good profit. One reason for this is because people don't want to keep a bad trade over lunch time, as waiting this long often means they will have a harder time getting out of their bad trade.

This is also around the time people are getting ready for lunch, which occurs between 11:00 am and 2:15 pm. There might be one last spike of people cashing out their stocks before lunch. This is known to be one of the quietest times for the stock market. If you are an all-day trader, you will probably spend your time taking your lunch break and then coming back to do some more research. If you are new to trading in the stock market, this would be the perfect opportunity to educate yourself a bit more on day trading, other forms of trading, or investing in general. After all, day trading might be a stepping stone for you in your new career.

The Afternoon Market

After the lunch time, you will begin to see more activity in the stock market. People will not only be looking for new trades, but they will also be paying attention to any major trends. By 2:00 pm, the trends of the day are pretty much set. Therefore, you are able to find stocks that might be good for using strategies where you look for breakouts or breakdowns.

Around 3:00 in the afternoon is the last strong push for traders. It is during this time, where day traders are working on selling the rest of their stocks or, if they also get into swing trading, looking to see if their stocks would make good swing stocks. Because traders are needed to get rid of stocks, you will see some traders make profits and you will see others lose money. The more you delve into the world of day trading, you will find yourself on both sides daily. Remember, as a day trader you are going to lose some as much as you win some. As long as you follow the strategies outlined in this book and do what you can to limit risk, you shouldn't find yourself losing out on too much money.

The closer you get to 4:00 Eastern Time, the more you will find people closing out or canceling unfulfilled orders. It is important to make sure that all orders that do not get filled are closed because these can be filled with you realizing it, which can quickly make you lose money.

After the Stock Market Closes

Just because the stock market closed doesn't mean you are completely done with the day. Of course, this is completely your choice. While some traders will close out and be done, others will close out and then spend some time, generally not more than an hour, analyzing how their day went. If you are new to the stock market world, it wouldn't be a bad idea to get into this habit as you will be able to learn a lot about your decisions, notice any mistakes, and see what you can change to become a better trader.

Trading Journal

Some traders often write in their trading journal during this time. This is a great technique to help traders learn more about their progress and how they run their business. Furthermore, it can help them realize where they need more experience, where they are becoming experienced, and any changes that need to be made to their routines and strategies. You can also take this journal to your advisor or broker to show him or her where you are sitting as a trader.

While there are many benefits to keeping a trading journal, one of the biggest benefits is being able to see details of your trades that your reports won't tell you. For example, you will be able discuss what the market conditions were like when you took part in a certain trade, which is something that you just can't get from your brokerage report. You can discuss if you found yourself distracted, which caused you to make a mistake, or you can discuss anything analysis about your trades or the stock market in general. On top of this, you are always able to go back to your journal at any time. You can look back to see what changes you have made over the year, what you have learned, what you still need to work on, and what environmental conditions affect your trading. For example, you could find that you don't trade as well during the later winter months or that you trade better during the spring.

However, you don't have to write in a journal if you don't want to. You could take a screenshot of your trades throughout the day or review your charts. This will allow you to keep this information in your company and go back to it whenever you want, just like a journal. Of course, you can always take time to make notes about your screenshots as well by following these steps:

1. You will want to mark your start time with a text note or vertical line on your chart. This will allow you note if you started early, late, and what factors created this event.

2. You can make a text note of what happened before you started trading. For example, you can discuss the environment of the stock market or even of your personal life. Whether we work from home or not, there are always factors in our personal lives that can make work a bit more challenging from time to time. These can be important factors for you to note as they can change the way you handled your trades that day.

3. Continue to make text notes and lines on your graphs. Of course, you want to do this in a way where they won't distract you when you go back to look at the graph. Remember, you are doing this to help you in the future so you want to do what you can to limit any obstacles that might make you lose track of the chart in the future.

4. Make notes on the reasons you weren't trading. For example, did you not trade during a specific time because you felt the stock market was too unstable or because of the news you read about a certain company?

You will want to make sure to review your journal often. This will help you learn and grow as a trader. You will not only be able to notice the areas that need more research or work but you will also be able to notice your strengths. You can continue to build on your strengths and address any weaknesses you have pinpointed.

One of the biggest things to note about keeping a journal is the need to find your routine and stick to it. Take time to think about if you want to use a mix of graphs and a written words, just graphs, or just a written journal. This is a personal preference, however, many experienced traders who keep journals often state that the graphs are incredibly helpful, as you can actually see what you did that day instead of just reading a description.

Bonus Section: How to Manage Your Time as a Day Trader

Welcome to the special bonus section which will discuss special techniques to help you learn how to manage your time as a day trader. Whether you are a part-time or full-time trader, it is important to learn how to manage your time so you can become a successful trader. There are many ways that you can focus on managing your time better and I will discuss several of these here. However, before I begin, it is essential that I take some time to remind you that incorporating these techniques into your day won't happen overnight. It will take time and you will have to have self-control when you focus on integrating these techniques into your day trading career.

Find a Strategy That Can Become a Part of Your Lifestyle and Personality

No matter who you are, you have a different personality and lifestyle than any other trader you will get to know during your career, including your mentor. This is why it is important that you need to get to know yourself before you start to incorporate day trading into your life. It doesn't matter if you only trade part-time or if you decide to take on trading as your new full-time career. The fact of the matter is that you have to find enough time in your day to get in all the details of trading, from the pre-trading analysis to the post-trading analysis, without becoming too exhausted in your daily life.

In order to do this, you have to sit down and think about how much time you can spend trading each day. You need to first do enough research to learn about all the hard work that goes into trading and then you will need to look at your own schedule. If you already have a full-time job, you will probably want to decide if you are going to leave this job and start trading full-time. However, you also want to note that you might not be able to make your income from your current position right away as a trader. Therefore, you will need to take a good look at your finances to see where you can come up with the best solution.

However, finding a strategy that works for you goes farther than just becoming a full or part-time trader. It goes into deciding what trading strategy you will use. For example, if you know you are a patient person, then you will be able to handle a strategy where you could end up waiting for the right opportunity to trade until the end of the day. Of course, you also need to keep in mind that this means you will have to be a full-time trader. However, if you plan to be a part-time trader or you realize you need to work on your patience, you will probably follow a strategy that doesn't require as much patience and wait time.

Don't Try to Force Time

When you first start day trading, you will find that no matter how much research and planning you did, you will continue to struggle with finding the best system. You will be focusing on trial and error until you start to find something that works for you. While you are going through this time, it is important to remember that you should never try to force yourself to create more time in your day to work on trading. Some people might do this because they want to conduct more research for their trades. This can quickly make you feel exhausted and drained. Therefore, it is best to stick within the timeframe you have set for yourself in your trading plan.

Another way people tend to force time is by getting into a trade where they don't feel right. They might not feel like this is the best trade because the strategy they use might not work or they might feel there is too much risk. However, for various reasons (such as the amount of capital they could gain from the trade), people feel that they should continue to take on the stock. This is forcing time because it compels you to take time for something you don't feel comfortable with. Remember, it is important to feel comfortable with any trade you make. This includes how you spend your time.

Keep Away from the Distractions

Distractions can cause you to mismanage your time. This is a common occurrence, especially when traders work from home. While some have a problem looking away from their television, others try to take on day trading because they are trying to make a little extra money while staying home with their children. Both of these situations can become distractions. Of course, there are ways you can limit how often your television or surfing the internet can distract you. There aren't as many options for a stay-at-home parent to find ways to limit the time they need to spend with their children.

Therefore, when it comes to limiting distractions, it is important to limit them in a way that your lifestyle allows for. Maybe you decide to become a part-time trader and only focus on trading when your children are sleeping or spending time with a friend or at daycare. You might also decide that it might be best to just do what research you can while your children are young and then get into trading once they start school.

When it comes to other forms of home distractions, such as television, surfing the internet, being able to go outside on a whenever you want to, etc. you might have to find ways to combat these distractions through self-control techniques. For example, you might need to set up an office away from a television or you might have to shut off your phone and leave it in another room while you are working.

Because distractions take time away from your task, it is important that you take control of your distractions as soon as possible. You do not want to find yourself losing stocks because you made a mistake trading while you were watching a movie.

Find a Way to Systematically Learn All the Information You Need to

There is a lot of information when it comes to trading. Not only do you have to take part in classes, but you also have to continue to do your own research on your stocks, learn your strategy, learn the various patterns, and much more. This can all become a big challenge, especially when the human brain can only hold so much new information at one time. Therefore, you will need to find a system that works for you when you are learning all the valuable information of day trading.

Unfortunately, I can't just outline the best system for you to use. This is going to be something that you will have to try yourself. On top of this, you might have to try several techniques or combine a variety of techniques in order to help yourself discover the best method for learning and remembering all the information you need to. When it comes to this, you want to remember to be patient. Furthermore, you can help find the best way for you to retain the information by figuring out the best ways you learn. For example, a lot of people learn through flashcards. If you are one of these learners, you might find that flashcards of the terminology you will review in the next chapter, or flashcards explaining the different strategies or graphs, will be helpful for you.

Always Make Time to Look at the Charts

When you are looking to create your time management schedule, it is important to note that you should mark down everything you need to analyze throughout your day. Not only do you want to mark down time for your pre-trading analysis, but you also want to mark down time that will allow you to look at various stock charts throughout your day and during your post-trading analysis. All of these factors are very important and take time, especially when you are a beginner and just learning about day trading. Therefore, for a while, it might be best to allow yourself more time to look at charts than other day traders allow themselves. Remember, as you start to develop your skill and understand the profession better, you will be able to go back and create a different time management schedule.

Chapter 13: Understanding the

Terminology

No matter what type of trader or investor you are, you will run into a lot of terminology that is new to you in the stock market world. I have compiled a list of some of the most common terms and provided simple meanings to help you continue your education in your new career.

Trend line – This is the line that connects the lows and highs to show whether a stock is increasing or decreasing in price. It is important to note that there can be more than one trendline for a stock.

Breakout – This happens when a price hasn't moved much for a period of days. For example, the stock has fluctuated between $9 and $10 for five days but then changes in pattern. This pattern is known as a breakout and can mean the stock can quickly become profitable.

False breakout – This occurs when a trader believes there will be a break out due to the pattern, but the stock doesn't continue to rise in price.

Arbitrage – This occurs when you take advantage of the price difference between markets.

Short trade – This refers to a stock that you can sell without owning it but then turn around a buy it for a lower price.

Long trade – This refers to a stock a trader buys because he or she hopes the price will increase.

Initial Public Offering – This is when a company decides to make money by selling a certain number of their shares in the market.

Dividend – This is a certain amount of money that a company will send to a shareholder during certain times of the year. It could be sent monthly, quarterly, or annually.

Blue chip stocks – These are stocks held by some of the best companies, such as Target and Walmart, which have a history of success and offer dividends.

Capital gains – The amount of money you make when you sell or trade a commodity.

Capital loss – The amount of money you lose when you sell or trade a stock.

Watchlist – A list of stocks or other commodities that is observed on a daily basis, generally in the morning, for chances in trading.

Conclusion

Congratulations! You have now completed one of the most comprehensive books about day trading for beginners. You should now feel ready to begin your new career as a day trader.

By now, you have gained more insight on day trading than you had when you picked up this book. Not only do you know what day trading is, but you know what a typical day is like for a trader. On top of this, you know a few bonus tips on how to manage your time, you know several common mistakes that day traders make (that you can now avoid), and you know the right mindset that you have to work towards in order to reach success as a trader.

Of course, you have also learned different day trading strategies and platforms that are commonly used. You have learned about the steps you need to take before you begin trading, such as creating your business or trading plan and all the research that goes into learning about the profession. You have also read about creating a watchlist, how important your trading plan is, and how to execute your trading plan when you begin your day trading journey.

This book also touched on a few stocks that many day traders look at throughout their day and factors that will help you in choosing the best stocks for you. Furthermore, you have learned that there are different types of brokers, how to find the best broker, and the rights you have when it comes to working with your chosen broker.

Although this is a comprehensive beginner's book, your research and learning journey as a day trader is not over. There are many other resources that you can look into, including the resources included in this book. I want to see you succeed in your day trading career and, therefore, I hope that you will take the information from this book with you as you begin your journey. Best wishes and happy trading!

Swing Trading for Beginners

The Complete Guide on How to Become a Profitable Trader Using These Proven Swing Trading Techniques and Strategies. Includes Stocks, Options, ETFs, Forex, & Futures

Introduction

First, I want to thank you for choosing this book to help you learn about swing trading. The goal of this book is to help you along your journey to becoming a successful swing trader. As I will discuss later, it is important to make sure that you do your research before and after you start your career as a swing trader. I am honored that you selected this book to help you learn about swing trading. As you will be able to see from the bibliography, I have selected dozens of educational resources for the research of this book. It is my hope that my book helps ease your research by giving you the information you need to begin your journey.

In the first chapter, I will give you an introduction to financial trading. This chapter will not only describe the difference between investing and trading but it will also give you three key concepts of financial trading, such as asking yourself what you are trading and who is completing the trade. I will then explain the different types of brokers and what rights you have when you find a broker who you want to work with. I will then end this chapter by discussing the two stock market conditions that you will get to know as a swing trader.

In chapter two, I will give you a thorough introduction to what swing trading is and what it isn't. I will briefly discuss why you will want to pick swing trading over day trading. I want to focus on this because people are often confused between swing trading and day trading. I will then discuss the different stock trends, how you can decide what the right stocks are for you, and then give you a few ideas on what type of stock you can look out for as a swing trader.

In chapter three, I will look at the various financial instruments that are a part of the investing world. For example, I will take a look at options, ETFs, futures, and stocks.

Chapter four will look at how you need to treat swing trading like a professional business and not a hobby, which is often a mistake for beginners. In this chapter, I will help you walk through the process of how you will start to build your swing trading career. First, I will discuss how you can establish your own business plan, which is often referred to as a trading plan. I will then discuss how you have to make sure to set your daily schedule and how important this is to stick to. Of course, I will end out the chapter by discussing how you want to take your new career seriously, but not too serious because you don't want to become burnt-out due to working too hard as a swing trader.

In chapter five, you will learn the art of swing trading. In this chapter, I will discuss the beginning steps that you will take; such as research, finding a broker, simulation trading, and making swing trading your new career. For the second half of this chapter, I will discuss what a swing trader's day looks like. You will learn how your typical day will go from the time you start your work day to the time you close when the stock market closes, and how you need to perform your post-trading analysis.

Chapter six takes a look at the various trading strategies that you will run into as a swing trader. I first begin this chapter by discussing trend following, which is not only a strategy but one of the most important factors when it comes to analyzing your reports. You will then learn about short interest, news playing, breakouts and breakdowns, and a couple of others.

In chapter seven, I will look at the art of selling short. While this is a strategy that you will use when the stock market is facing poor conditions, I have given this strategy its own chapter because it is often confusing to many beginners. Therefore, I wanted to spend more time explaining short selling in a way that you are most likely to understand. Of course, I will not only discuss the process of short selling, but I will also look at the risks associated with this strategy.

While all of the chapters in this book are important to beginners, chapter eight is often one of the most used chapters in any beginner's guide. This chapter focuses on a variety of tips for beginners. These tips come from other experienced traders who, through their blogs, articles, or books, wanted to give you helpful information so you can become a successful swing trader. This chapter will discuss tips such as joining an online community, making education a top priority, becoming flexible, and making sure you have the right mindset.

Of course, because I took time to discuss tips for beginners, I also wanted to make sure you received a good amount of information regarding mistakes that other swing traders have shared. While there are countless mistakes that swing traders make, it is part of the job and something that will never go away, I only discuss a few mistakes. A couple of the mistakes that I will look at are how many new traders have unrealistic expectations about swing trading and how many don't pay attention to their mental health.

Through my research for this book, I came across and educational site about swing trading which discussed the 11 commandments of swing trading. As I was reading through these commandments, I realized that this is some of the most valuable information I had read about the topic. Therefore, I included this in the book. Some of the commandments are how you always make sure to have a clear plan, you need to work to put the odds in your favor, and you always need to remember to look at long-term charts.

In trading, there are two main forms of analysis. The first one is fundamental analysis, which I discuss in chapter eleven. This chapter focuses on a variety of fundamental valuables that you can use when you are analyzing and explains what fundamental analysis is. The second form of analysis is called technical analysis. This is the bigger form of analysis between the two, which means that this book focuses more on technical analysis than fundamental analysis. When looking at technical analysis, which is chapter twelve, I explain what you will study through the technical analysis lens.

Chapter thirteen takes a look at how you can limit your risk as a swing trader. It is important to note that you will never be able to eliminate risk completely. However, you can use a variety of techniques in order to limit your risks as much as possible when you trade stocks. Some of the strategies I will focus on are how to keep your emotions in check, determining your stop-loss amount, how you shouldn't trade alone (especially as a beginner), and how you should follow the 1% rule.

Finally, chapter fourteen will look at how psychology and swing trading are important to each other. In this chapter, I will discuss how you need to focus on keeping mentally healthy, so you can become the best swing trader possible. For example, I will discuss how you need to make sure you get enough sleep, how you need to focus on the positive, and how you need to practice self-control.

Through all these chapters, you will receive one of the most in-depth looks at swing trading on the market. You will not only learn what swing trading is, but you will also learn techniques, tips, and how psychology is a part of swing trading.

Chapter 1: Introduction to Financial Trading

While all the chapters of this book are equally important, it is important to start with this chapter because you get the basics of trading in general. What I mean is, you will want to read this chapter before you read any other chapter in this book. There are many people who will often skip to a chapter they feel they are interested in or need the most. For this book, it is important this is the first chapter you read, as it will prepare you for further reading.

At the base of financial trading is the hope that you make a profit through buying and selling stocks, currencies, or other commodities. There are many types of financial trading. This book focuses on swing trading, but there is also day trading, position trading, and momentum trading. While they each focus on the same basic idea of making a profit, they are all a little different in the trading world.

Before I go any farther, I should mention a myth about trading. This myth states that the only people who can take on trading as a profession are the people who have significant wealth. Fortunately, with today's technology, brokers who are willing to work with people who don't meet the $25,000 minimum balance rule and other factors, anyone can become a trader. While you can't open a trading account with no money, you do not need thousands of dollars to put into your account at first. You can start with a few thousand and then work your way up. If you are a trader who starts with only a few thousand, you will want to make sure that you find the best broker to work with you. Furthermore, you will want to make sure that the broker has relatively cheap fees.

Trading vs. Investing

Before you get into trading, you should know the difference between trading and investing. One reason I want to discuss this is because there are a lot of people who get into trading and realize it is different from investing. In reality, they wanted to start investing their money and not focus on trading. Another reason is because trading isn't for everyone. While anyone can take on trading, some people are more interested in investing. On top of this, there are people who don't have the patience to focus on trading or they find the job to be too stressful.

This is not to say that you need to decide right now if you are meant to be an investor or a trader. You should definitely look at all your options and even try out simulation trading before deciding. simulation trading is when you start to trade financial instruments but complete the process without money.

While investing is seen as a long-term approach to building your wealth, trading is seen as a short-term approach which allows you to maximize returns. Returns are the money that you will receive daily or during certain times of the year. In a sense, it is the income you have generated during trading.

Investors will often build their wealth by starting a retirement account or using the buy and hold stock method. One of the most popular buy and hold investors of 2019 is Warren Buffet, who became a millionaire through investing. Investors don't tend to pay attention to the daily trends of financial investments. For example, they will not decide to sell a stock because the price decreased. In fact, some investors don't pay attention to the daily price of stocks at all and, therefore, might not even realize the price of the stock decreased. If they do notice, they don't worry about it because they know that the price will increase over time. It is important to note that you might already be an investor. Anyone who pays into a 401K or has a savings account is considered to be an investor.

Traders build their wealth by purchasing and selling stocks over a short period of time. Day traders will buy commodities in the morning and then sell them at the best opportunity they see that same day. Swing traders will hold on to their financial instruments for a little longer. Sometimes they have them for a few days and other times up to a couple weeks. Another type of trader is known as a position trader, who tends to hold their instruments anywhere from a few months to a year or so. Scalp traders are similar to day traders in that they never hold their stocks overnight (which would turn them into swing stocks); however, they also don't hold the stock for most of the trading day. Instead, scalp traders will only hold their stocks from seconds and into a few minutes.

Key Concepts of Financial Trading

What Are You Trading?

One of the first questions you should ask yourself is what financial instruments, such as stocks, bonds, or ETFs are being traded. Even though you will always want the same outcome, which is a profit, you will want to make sure you understand the financial instrument that is being traded because you will handle each one differently.

Who is Doing the Trading?

This is an important question because you need to be able to identify the trader. You are the trader or is someone else doing the trading? You need to be able to identify the financial instrument part of a company, government institution, or person. This is important because you have to be able to identify the commodities which move the most. When this happens, they are known to be part of a volatile market which bring both positives and negatives. On the positive side, financial instruments from volatile markets will give you bigger capital gains, which is when you make a profit. On the other side, they also bring more risk.

Where Are You Completing the Trade?

There are two places where you can complete a trade. The first one is known as over-the-counter, which is like when you trade a CFD with an institution. The second place is known as an exchange, such as the New York Stock Exchange. These are often completed through an online marketplace.

How Are Stocks Traded?

The days of shares needing to be traded in the building of the New York Stock Exchange or London Stock Exchange are gone. While many people still work in these buildings, it is more common for people to take in over-the-counter stock exchanging. This type of exchanging is what you do when you sit in front of your computer and use a platform to buy and sell financial instruments. With this type of trading, everything you do is recorded electronically which is a huge advantage for any trader. Because of this, you are able to screenshot all of your transactions and make notes on them, so you can look back at them in the future. This is known as post-trading analysis and will be discussed later.

It is important to realize that when you buy a stock, you are not buying a stock directly from the company. You are buying the stock from the shareholder. The company sold the stock before you purchased the stock from the shareholder. This is the exact same thing as when you sell a stock. You are not part of the company selling a stock, you are a shareholder who is selling the stock to the new shareholder.

Finding a Broker

While all traders won't have a broker, it is important that you find the right broker for you when you are starting your swing trading career. A broker is the person who will not only help you perform your trades, but will also give you an advice, reading material, help you with research, and help you in any other way he or she can as a broker.

The biggest rule when it comes to finding a broker is you have to find one that you can trust and respect. You need to remember, you will not only be giving this broker your important bank information, but you will start your new career alongside this broker. You will be getting advice, learning how to make trades, letting your broker help you decide what trades to make, and so much more.

There are different types of brokers.

1. Interactive Broker

Unfortunately, if you can't make the $25,000 minimum amount pattern day trader rule then you can't use an interactive broker. However, if you can make this rule, then you might want to look to see if this is the type of broker for you because they tend to be the cheapest with fees. For example, they usually only charge about $1 per trade, but they will have other fees associated with this amount which all brokers will have.

2. Sure Traders

Sure Traders are brokers who will help people who cannot make the pattern day trader rule. However, they also tend to be a little more expensive. On average, they charge about $10 trading fee and could charge other fees on top of this. Sure Traders are known to be some of the most helpful brokers for beginners, especially traders who take on the swing trading career.

3. Full-Service Brokers

Full-Service brokers are ones who many people feel go above and beyond their job. While they are not the most popular among traders, they are a great source of help for swing traders. They will often be the brokers you want to pick if you are more interested in learning as much as you can through your broker. Unfortunately, because they give the whole package with their service, they tend to be some of the most expensive brokers.

4. Discount Brokers

Discount brokers are similar to the interactive broker as they are known to be extremely cheap. However, they won't always work with traders who have under $25,000 in their account. Discount brokers also tend to specialize with traders and don't often work with people who are interested in investing for more than a couple of years.

Make Sure You Understand Your Rights

No matter how well you trust your broker, you should always remember that you have rights. There are several rights that many traders and investors are not aware of when it comes to their relationship with their broker. The following list is of the most important rights you should remember when you start working with your broker.

- You have the right to look up your broker's historical professional information. While you might have to call your county or state offices, you are guaranteed the right to know if your potential broker has been cited with any illegal activity or any other customers have filed a complaint against your broker.

- If your broker does not give you the information you request, you have the right to go to your broker's supervisor to request the information. If you still don't receive any information from the supervisor, you have the right to go above the supervisor to receive the information. This might mean that you go to the company's headquarters or you reach out to your state agency.

- You have the right to receive all reports and correspondence in writing.

- You have the right to understand all the trades your broker is making on your behalf. You also have the right to make the final decision when it comes to trading.

- You have the right to be informed of any new information that details your stocks and trading portfolio.

- You have the right to ask any questions, so you can completely understand all of the trading information which is given to you.

Bull vs Bear Market

There are dozens of new trading terms that you will learn along your journey and one of the most common terms are bull and bear. These terms are two types of markets which focus on the current conditions within the stock market. They will often help you in deciding if you should take on a trade or not.

Bull Market

When the conditions of the market are doing well, it is referred to as a bull market. This means that not only are the stock market trends on the rise, but unemployment is low, and most people tend to not struggle as much financially. For a trader, bull markets can make it easier to pick stocks because the majority of the stocks are doing well.

Even though the conditions are great when it comes to the bull market doesn't mean that there aren't dangers associated with this type of market. One of the biggest problems with bull markets is known as a bubble. What happens is things seem to be going so well with trading that many traders will over evaluate the positive conditions. Basically, the stock market prices get too high. This can cause the conditions to not follow in their traditional manner and soon the good conditions will burst.

Bear Market

The bear market is the exact opposite of the bull market. In a bear market, the conditions aren't great as unemployment will be high and the stock market trends will be on a downward spiral. The biggest problem for traders when it comes to a bear market is that it is riskier for them to take on stocks. Of course, this doesn't mean that they stop trading. Instead, they are just become more cautious of the stocks they pick and do their best to find ones that will turn a decent profit.

Some traders during this time might stick to blue-chip stocks. These are stocks that are shares from the most powerful companies you can think of today, such as Target, Walmart, Apple, Amazon, and Microsoft. However, if these aren't your targeted stocks or you are not comfortable taking on these types of stocks, it is best to remain in your comfort zone, especially during bear market conditions.

When faced with the bear market, most traders will do something called short selling. This is when they hold a stock for the shortest time possible as it will give them a more decent profit, or at least they won't lose as much money. With short selling, traders don't actually buy the stocks. Instead, they borrow the stocks and then sell them. Unfortunately, this can be very risky business for beginners. Furthermore, short selling carries its own set of risks.

One of the biggest reasons why short selling isn't meant for beginners is because it can become very tricky. In reality, you are often gambling with your money as you work towards trying to make a profit through borrowing and selling. There are very specific times that you need to find in order to short sell and make the best profit. Of course, any trader is able to accomplish short selling and become profitable. Like with any other factor in trading, you will just need to make sure that you do your research, speak with your advisor, and understand the process.

Chapter 2: What is Swing Trading?

Some people tend to confuse swing trading with other types of trading. It is important to know that each type of trading is different. For example, when you are a day trader, you will buy and sell stocks in one day. You do not hold stocks overnight. If you do decide to hold a stock overnight, you turn it into a swing trading stock. Swing traders tend to hold their stocks for a few days, however, they also have a limited time frame. While the average swing trader might hold on to stocks for a couple of weeks, some might hold on to stocks for as long as a couple of months. Typically, if a trade is held longer than this, it isn't considered a swing trade anymore. However, there are always exceptions to every rule.

Why Swing Trading Over Day Trading?

While you can take up any type of trading, many people feel that swing trading is better than day trading. Lately, day trading has become a popular topic because it can be completed within a few minutes to an hour or so. However, this is also one reason that people tend to turn away from day trading.

Other than the different time frames between day trading and swing trading, many people chose swing trading because they feel it is less demanding. There is a lot of truth to this as day traders often feel a bit more stress as they have to pay such close attention to the stocks in order to trade them in just the right moment, which can be within minutes, in order to make the best profit. While everyone has to focus on just the right moment to trade so they receive the best profit, day traders need to close out their stocks the same day they purchase them, otherwise they will most likely lose money.

Furthermore, day traders have to watch several screens throughout the day. Of course, much of this depends on how many stocks they take on. However, this tends to become very challenging, especially for beginners. When it comes to swing traders, they have to watch several screens closely, but not to the intensity of day traders.

Another reason people chose swing trading over day trading is that it's easier to be a part-time trader. While there are part-time day traders, many feel that it is a full-time job if you want to gain the best profits from the career.

When it comes to swing trading, you are given a few days and up to a couple of months to watch your stocks and find the best time to make your highest profit. Because of this, people don't feel as much pressure.

Swing traders also don't have to worry about making sure they have the greatest equipment and worry about all the algorithms that go into day trading. Instead, swing traders can get a platform and perform their own trades, once they learn, on a typical computer. Of course, you will still need to make sure that your computer is reliable and have the same high-speed internet that day traders need.

Stock Trends

Like with other types of trading, you will need to heavily focus on analysis in order to try to gain an idea of where the stock trend is heading next. For example, if you look at a stock's trend history for the last couple of months and noticed it has been in an upward trend, you might assume that this upward trend is going to continue. However, you will also need to look at other features in order to officially determine if this is the best stock for you. Thankfully, trends tend to repeat themselves which is why people can easily predict where the stock is going to go. However, this doesn't mean that trends don't quickly change.

There are times during an upward trend when you will see what traders call a pull-back. This is when the trend of the stock drops down but then rises back up later.

Pull-backs also repeat. However, if they are successful, they will have higher lows and higher highs than the previous pull back.

This is a pattern that you will want to notice as a swing trader because, as long as the stock will work with your strategy and everything else matches up with your trading plan, it is the trend you want to find. The best time to buy one of these stocks is when is during a pull-back. This is when the stock will be at a low price, which means your profit will be greater, once the stock shoots up to a higher price and you can sell it at the right time.

Another type of trend that you have to understand as a trader is the downward trend. This trend is the opposite of the upward trend but still can give you a profit, if you understand when to buy and sell the stocks. The best time to buy the stock on a downward trend is when the stock is at a low point. Of course, you will want to sell the stock when it is on its way back up from the lowest point, a term which is known as pull-up.

While this might sound pretty simple, it can actually be a little harder to understand and find the best time to buy and sell. The biggest way you will find the best time to buy and sell the stock is through technical analysis, which I will discuss later in this book. The basis of technical analysis is you will be able to identify the patterns because you analyze the historical trend and information of the stock. Through technical analysis, you will receive tools that will help you isolate and identify the patterns.

How to Decide on the Right Stocks

One of the most difficult decisions you will run into as a swing trader, or any trader, is deciding what stocks are the best to trade. There are a lot of factors that go into this from the strategies you use to your lifestyle. Unfortunately, I cannot give you a guide that strictly tells you what stocks you should go out and take on. However, I will try to give you information that can help you make your own decision.

One of the key features to look at when you are choosing your stock is to find a stock that comes from a large capital company. These companies might be part of the blue-chip stocks, such as Amazon and Walmart. However, they don't have to be. In general, large capital companies tend to have at least $5 billion dollars. These stocks are generally the most sought-after stocks in the market, which help make them highly tradable. They are also known to give you a good profit because they have a long history of success.

The trend is another key feature that you want to pay attention to. You want to make sure that the stock has been going in the same direction for a few days, if not a few weeks. This will help you to note that, chances are, the stock will continue this trend. Of course, if you decide to take on the stock, you want to continue to closely watch the stock because you never truly know when the stock will switch directions and you can find yourself losing capital instead of gaining.

Ideas on Good Swing Trading Stocks

While I cannot tell you exactly what stocks to get, I can give you an idea, so you can at least start to look at some stocks that many swing traders put into their basket.

Netflix

Netflix is considered to be one of the top swing trade stocks for 2019. Of course, this stock has a higher price than most swing trade stocks, which is often harder for beginners to take advantage of. However, if you have enough finances to put into Netflix, many traders feel it is a good option. Furthermore, because of the successful history of Netflix, many people believe that the stock isn't going to see a huge downward trend anytime soon.

Amazon

Amazon is similar to Netflix. It is believed to be one of the biggest swing trading stocks for 2019 because of its successful history. Like Netflix, Amazon is also on the more expensive side, however is known to give great returns.

MKS Instruments

In 2019, most tech companies are some of the top stocks that people take on as swing traders, day traders, and investors. MKS Instruments is based out of Massachusetts and has been on an upward trend for a while.

Chapter 3: Finding a Suitable Market

One of the most difficult parts of swing trading, especially for a beginner, is finding the best market for you. This includes what type of financial instruments you want to focus on when it comes to trading. There are a variety of financial instruments; such as ETFs, futures, options, currencies, cryptocurrencies, and stocks. As a beginner, it is important to try to find one financial instrument that you are comfortable with. This chapter will go into the different types of financial instruments, so you can gain a better sense of which instrument is the best for your trading lifestyle. While discussing the various types of financial instruments, I will also give you some of the pros and cons that go with these instruments. The goal for this chapter is to help you decide whether you are going to focus on stock, currencies, ETFs, or other another financial instrument.

Of course, while you want to pick one financial instrument, this does not mean that you can't do more research to see if you have chosen the right instrument. For example, you might feel that stocks are your best option because you hear the most about them. However, once you start to trading with stocks, you begin to think that you might be better of trading currencies. You can then switch your financial instrument to see if currencies are a better fit for you.

Sometimes, following the guideline of trial and error is the best way to help you develop yourself as a trader. It is important to realize that you should establish your own trading personality. While you will follow the advice of others, such as people in your online community and your broker, you should still make sure to take time to figure out what is right for you. Many beginners have felt uncomfortable as a swing trader because they were following what other traders were doing instead of learning about their trading personality. If you want to become a successful swing trader, you will focus on developing your trading personality instead of following someone else.

Selecting a Financial Instrument to Trade

Stocks

Stock are probably the most common financial instrument that people think of when they start their trading career. In fact, most people probably believe that this is the financial instrument they will be trading. Part of this is because of the popularity. However, another part is because they really don't realize how many financial instruments there are when it comes to trading.

When people talk about stocks in the trading community, they will often refer to them as shares. There are several ways you can handle shares. Of course, you can decide to trade shares using the swing trading technique or you can decide to invest your stocks with the buy and hold method. Whatever you choose to do (you might change your mind once you truly start trading) it is important to remember that you need to continue your research and get to know as much as possible about trading stocks in the market. This not only means that you have to learn about stocks, but it also means that you have to learn about the stock market in general. In reality, this goes for any type of financial instrument you decide to focus on.

Because stocks are so popular, it is important to look carefully at your research. For example, you might find valuable information about a stock but realize the website is focusing on investing stocks instead of trading them. While you can learn about the details of a stock through this resource, you won't want to spend your time focusing on investing stocks when you are looking into trading. The main reason for this is because, as I have mentioned earlier, trading and investing are two different pieces of the stock market. When you invest, you hold the stock for a long period of time. In fact, there are many investors who focus on holding the stock for the rest of their life. But, when you are a swing trader, there is only a small window of time you will hold your stock. Therefore, you want to make sure that you are reading about the correct strategies and information to help you along your swing trading journey.

One of the biggest examples of running into information about stocks that won't be important to you as a swing trader is reading that you should not pay attention to the daily prices of the stock market. While this is valuable information for an investor who focuses on the buy and hold strategy, this is not valuable information for someone who is taking on swing trading. While you won't need to focus on every single price dip and rise like day traders do, unless you are trying to analyze a chart, you will need to pay close attention to the daily stock prices you have in your portfolio.

At the same time, you want to make sure that you are focusing on stocks that are within your target companies. For example, you might want to focus on blue-chip stocks. Therefore, if you find a stock that isn't considered blue-chip, you will want to move on.

One of the biggest downsides to choosing stocks is that each stock you take on will carry its own individual risk. This means that no matter what type of negative news comes about the company for a stock you hold, such as Google or Twitter, you will have the risk of losing money due to the negative news. However, there is a way to trade stocks without having to think of each stock carrying it's own risk and this is through ETFs.

ETFs

ETFs are known as Exchange-Traded Funds. When you think of ETFs you can picture a bunch of stocks in one basket. What this group of stocks or other securities you decide to trade do is analyze the underlying index of the fund. There are a variety of ETFs. For example, you can choose an ETF that follows more of a target, such as retail companies or you could choose an ETF that has more variety within its basket. While you are looking at different ETFs, you want to keep in mind the same rules and guidelines for yourself that you do for stocks or any other type of financial instrument. While ETFs used to be focused more towards stocks, they can now focus on bonds, currencies, and even looking into cryptocurrencies.

One of the biggest pros to ETFs is you are able to have variety through purchasing one ETF because it is made up of different securities. Many people believe that this can save you money because if you decided to purchase the stocks in the ETF separately, you would be spending more money. For example, if you are interested in stocks that focus on space, you can look for an ETF that has this target instead of having to purchase a dozen or more separate stocks. In fact, most ETFs can hold hundreds of stocks.

Another positive of ETFs is you don't have to worry so much if one of the company's securities start to fall because of negative press as the other securities will help balance out the fall. Therefore, you might not even notice that price drop from one security. Because of this, many traders feel that ETFs are a good risk management instrument.

The price also tends to be more of a positive when it comes to ETFs. While most people believe that they will be expensive because they hold so many securities from different companies, this method of thinking isn't true. In fact, you might find that many ETFs are cheaper than some of the most popular blue-chip stocks on the market. On top of this, some ETFs might have a blue-chip stock within them.

Diversification is one of the terms that you will often run into as a trader. Diversification basically means that you have a variety of stock or whatever type of financial instrument you decide to trade. This is another reason why many traders look at ETFs as they will offer diversification through their variety of stocks. However, many traders and investors feel that diversification can also be a negative in the stock world. While it is highly debated, some people feel that if you have too much

diversification in your account, then you can find
yourself struggling to manage some risks.

Currencies

Trading currencies is just like trading money when you
go on a vacation. For example, if you live in Canada and
you decide to travel to Europe, you will have to trade
your Canadian money in for Euros. In a sense, trading
currencies in the stock market works the same way. You
will always need to have two different currencies in order
to trade. You will also want to watch to see what the
value of the money is through a comparison. For
example, some currencies receive a higher value
compared to others while other currencies receive a
lower value.

Currency trades are completed in the Foreign Exchange
Market, which is known as forex. While this is a different
market, you will still want to make sure to follow the
same risk management techniques that you do when
trading in the stock market. For example, you will want
to make sure that you only trade a certain percentage of
your account amount, such as 1% (this will be discussed
later). You will also want to make sure that you take all
the time you need in order to learn about trading
currencies and the foreign exchange stock market.

One important piece of advice from many experienced
swing traders is that most of them agree that you should

not start out trading using currencies as your financial instrument. They really believe that after you use simulation trading, you should turn your attention to stocks as these are often considered to be a base in the trading world. Stocks have been around an incredibly long time, which often helps beginners as they are learning the guidelines, rules, and how to trade in general.

Cryptocurrencies

Cryptocurrencies are one of the newest types of financial instruments available to trade. They are similar to currencies, however they are often discussed as coins and have a variety of different coins. Some of the types of cryptocurrencies are Ethereum, Ripple, Bitcoin Lite, and Bitcoin.

Just like currencies, nearly every experienced trader will tell you that beginners should not start with cryptocurrencies. In fact, most would probably see a beginner start with currency over cryptocurrencies. There are a couple main reasons for this one, both of them dealing with how risky these types of financial instruments are.

First, cryptocurrencies are newer and this means that there isn't as much research completed on them. In fact, one of the main things that experienced traders who are including cryptocurrencies in their portfolio are working hard to make sure they note everything about their trades so they can help expand the research on this type of financial instrument.

Second, cryptocurrencies are known to have high risk. In fact, many believe that they are the most high risk financial instruments that you can trade and invest in. They tend to suffer more than any other instrument when it comes to negative press, governmental regulations, and are even more likely to be hacked. Because of this, many traders feel it is important that the people who take on cryptocurrencies are comfortable with high risk, won't allow their mental state to be affected by the risk, and can remain calm under stress so they can continue to think rationally when having to make a quick decision to trade.

Futures

Futures are a good way to start your trading career. This is one of the most popular financial instruments among day traders but are also great for beginners who are looking to become swing traders. When you think of a future, you can think of an agreement between two people. A future is basically a contract that states exactly when stock will be sold. Typically, the agreement states that the stock will only be sold at a specific price. For example, both parties could agree that if the stock reaches $5, then the stock is to be sold. However, the stock cannot be sold to the second party until the price of $5 is reached.

Many people feel that futures are a great way to learn about the stock market. It decreases risk because you are able to create a contract that states this stock will be sold at a certain price. Of course, before you decide to agree to the contract, you will do all the research you need to do and make sure, to the best of your abilities, that you will end up with capital gain instead of a loss with the price you choose. Many beginners who state that they used futures within their first couple of months as a trader say they were able to get some more hands-on experience and learn about the stock market as they took part in futures. On top of that, they were able to gain pretty good profits.

Options

In the basic sense, options are similar to futures in there is a contract between two parties that states when the stock can be sold. However, instead of just focusing on the price, the agreement also focuses on a specific date. Furthermore, in order for the stock to become an option, there are four requirements that are needed.

1. The owner of the stock needs to agree upon the price. This process is known as the strike price.

2. You need to know the stock that the option is being applied to, such as IBM or MasterCard.

3. When it comes to options, buying is referred to as call and selling is referred to as put.

4. You also need to have a date of expiration for the option.

Like with any other type of financial instrument, there are positives and negatives associated with options. It is important to remember that all trades carry some sort of risk, no matter how well you try to manage the risk. This means that you can exhaust yourself making sure you have used every risk management technique that you can use and still have an amount of risk involved. Therefore, it is best to understand that sometimes you will lose on a trade and other times you will profit.

One negative side to options is the expiration date. If you hit the expiration date, then the agreement is considered to be worthless and you have taken a 100% loss on the stock. However, one of the positives of options is that you don't have to use a lot of capital in order to trade a high priced stock.

Chapter 4: Treat Swing Trading

Like a Business

One of the most important pieces of information to receive as you start on your journey is that you will become more successful as a swing trader if you treat it as a career and not just a hobby. You don't have to work full-time in order to believe that swing trading is a profession to be taken seriously. Some traders decide to work part-time because this is best for their lifestyle. For example, a stay-at-home parent will often become too distracted to focus on trading the whole day. When you take on trading full-time, you will usually be in front of your computer during the hours the New York Stock Exchange is open, which is about 9:30 am to around 4:00 pm Eastern time zone. This means, if you live in California, then you will start your day before 6:30.

Establish Your Business Plan

Because you should treat trading like a profession, it is important to follow a number of steps you would use when starting your own business. First, you will want to make sure you create a business or trading plan. This is a plan which will discuss all the details about your style as a trader. You will discuss your enter strategy, exit strategy, your pre-trading analysis, and your post-trading analysis.

What is a Business Plan?

Your business plan is going to be your comprehensive guide that will help you with your decisions as a swing trader. These are not only important because every business should have one but because they can help you make the best decision when you are faced with deciding if you should take on or sell a financial instrument. No matter how well you have researched swing trading or how long you have been a swing trader, when you are faced with a decision you can easily struggle to come up with a solution. This is when your trading plan will come in handy. You will focus on every aspect that goes with swing trading, including tips to help you focus on making the right decision and why.

It is important to evaluate your trading plan often. In fact, many traders state you should read through your trading plan during your pre-trading analysis. Other traders state that you should at least read through your plan and make any changes, if necessary, on a weekly basis. Whatever you decide to do, you want to make sure that you know your trading plan as well as you know anything else in trading. Even though you will be reading the plan often, you still want to make sure you have memorized the plan as this will help you when you are faced with a difficult decision.

Why You Need a Trading Plan?

Your trading plan has several advantages. First, it will help you make decisions when you are focusing on a trade. While you might feel that these decisions should be easy, there is a lot of analyzing and details that go into making a decision to take on a financial instrument. This means that when you are faced with a decision that you need to make within a minute or two, you can often become stressed or worried about your decision. Of course, this isn't something you want to do when it comes to trading as then you might make the decision with your emotions, which definitely isn't something you want to do as a trader. If you find yourself in this position, you can turn to your trading plan. This plan will walk you through your decision, so you are less likely to make any mistakes.

Set Your Schedule and Stick to It

I talk about establishing your schedule, I am not just talking about how long you will sit in front of your computer when you are trading. There is a lot of information which goes into creating your schedule.

First, you will want to decide if you are going to become a part-time or full-time swing trader. This will let you know how much time to set aside for your trading career. For example, if you are part-time, you might think about focusing on trading a couple of days during the week or trade in the mornings. However, if you are a full-time trader, you will probably want to stay close to your computer during the hours the stock market is open. Below are the pieces of your schedule you should make sure to include no matter how often you trade during the week.

Pre-Trading Analysis

You will want to make sure to include time for your pre-trading analysis, which is a part of your trading plan. This analysis typically takes place before the stock market opens; however, some traders will use the first half hour as their analysis time. For instance, if you want to make sure your analysis is complete by the time the stock market opens, you will want to make sure you are done with this part of your day by 9:30 Eastern time. This could mean that you start your day at 5:45 am or 6:00 am as it is a good idea to have at least a half hour for your pre-trading analysis. However, many traders state that beginners should allow themselves a bit more time because they are still learning the whole trading system. Therefore, it could take them more time to analyze the changes that occurred in the foreign stock market or the United States stock market overnight. On top of this, they might take more time reading the news.

The Market

Of course, you will want to make sure that your schedule includes the on goings of the stock market. For example, you will want to note that from about 9:30 am to around 10:00 am, the market is in volatile mode. This means that there are a lot of changes occurring in the market which makes it unstable. When the market is unstable, you typically do not want to make and purchases or sales. Most people tend to just sit back and watch the market or spend their time reading the news or doing some research.

Another time to note about the stock market is that from about 11:15 am to around 2:00 pm is when the market seems to have the lowest amount of activity. Many traders refer to this time as the stock market's lunch time. Before 11:00 am, many traders will end their day as they are only part-time. However, those who are full-time might continue to research or look for stocks until their lunch time.

Starting around 2:30 pm, the stock market will begin to pick up again. When this happens, you will start to see activity and, if you are planning on making a sale or trade, you will most likely start looking into that. This activity continues until the stock market closes around 4:00 pm.

Post-Trading Analysis

Post-trading analysis is just as important as pre-trading analysis. You want to make sure to make time for this every day and it will occur after you have completed your day. During your post trade analysis, you will reflect on your day and you can do this through a trading journal or by taking screenshots of your charts for any trades you made that day.

If you use a trading journal, you will want to make sure to note every detail you feel is necessary about the day. This not only includes any financial instruments you bought or sold but also why. You will want to focus on why you made the decision, what strategy you used, what factors contributed to this decision, you will want to discuss if you were distracted, what device you used (computer, phone, etc.), your capital gain or loss, and anything else. It is important to write down as much as you feel you will need to so when you can get a sense of where your strengths and weaknesses are. On top of this, you will be able to get to know yourself as a trader.

If you decide to take screenshots of your charts, you will want to make sure to make notes within your charts. You will want to find a spot where you won't become distracted and can still read the chart easily. You will want to make the same type of notes you do in your trading journal. Of course, you could always take screenshots of charts and also keep a trading journal. How you do your analysis is up to you.

Take Your New Career Seriously but Not Too Seriously

Before you get into swing trading, whether you are going to focus on it halftime or full-time, you want to make sure that you are 100% committed to the career. It is very important that you don't feel like this is something you just want to try because you are bored or want to see if you can make some extra money every month. However, if you do feel this way, it is best to start up part-time and go from there.

At the same time, you need to make sure that you don't fall into the trap of taking your job too seriously. While this might sound odd, it can happen and has happened to many people within their jobs. Typically, when people start taking their job too seriously, they start to let it consume their life and there is very little professional and personal life balance. In fact, what happens is people tend to put all their time and energy into their job that they reach a state of exhaustion.

Becoming exhausted from trading can happen to anyone, and it is a fairly common trait, especially for beginners. Part of this reason is because they don't understand how demanding trading really is. Therefore, when they first get into the business, they have not dedicated enough time for what they wanted to do. Of course, this can be easily fixed by creating more time for trading or taking on less stocks. But, at the same time, they could reach a state of exhaustion before they realize they took on too much.

How to Tell When You're Heading Towards a Burn-Out?

Becoming burned-out from you job can happen to anyone. In fact, most people feel that they reach a stage of burnout at least once throughout their professional career. It is important to note that if you start to feel burnt-out, it is best to take a step back or a break. If you continue to work at the pace you are going and become too exhausted, you can easily start to cause other work-related problems. For example, you can start performing poorly. When it comes to swing trading, you might find yourself making more mistakes and unable to read and analyze charts that you used to be able to understand easily.

Many people reach a state of burn-out simply because they feel their job is too stressful. In fact, stress is the main factor of becoming burned-out. This is a common problem for many people in the trading community because, even swing trading, can be demanding.

There are many basic signs for a person who is starting to become burnt-out from there job.

1. You have lost your motivation for your job.

One of the biggest signs that you are nearing or becoming burnt-out is you have lost motivation for your job. This can happen to any one and in any field, not just trading. In fact, you might have already felt this way in a previous job. When you lose motivation, you really begin to feel that you can't do the tasks that you once used to do. You might feel that you are too tired to perform the tasks (exhaustion is another sign of being burned-out). You might also feel that the tasks aren't worth your time or find yourself procrastinating.

2. You feel a lot of negative emotions.

Another sign that you are becoming burned-out is you feel more negatively towards your job than positively. You might find that you are easily irritated by your co-workers or even feel that you just want to be left alone. You might find yourself becoming easily frustrated at the simplest tasks you need to complete. Of course, you will want to remember that people generally feel a bit negative about parts of their job from time to time. If you find yourself feeling negatively occasionally, you might not be burnt-out. However, if you notice that you are more negative than you typically are, especially if you begin to become concerned over your mental health, then you are most likely burn-out.

3. Your job performance is suffering.

One of the biggest ways to notice that you are burnt-out is by looking at your previous job performance and comparing it to your current performance. If you found your performance is sloppier and you are not putting as much effort into your job duties, then you have most likely become burned-out.

4. Always thinking about work, even when you're not working.

While people usually think about the things they need to do at work when they are not on the clock, if you find yourself doing this often you could easily be at the burnt-out stage. In fact, part of the reason you might feel burned-out is because you think of your job when you should be focusing on other things to give yourself a better balance between work and home.

This is one downside when it comes to working from home. People who are used to working in an office and then start to work from home can often find themselves working longer hours or thinking about work more. One reason for this is because it's more convenient for them to get to their office as it might just be down the hall. Furthermore, if you are a trader, you might trade through your desktop, which you use throughout your day for various reasons. This is why it is important to make sure you have some type of work schedule that you stick to when you work from home.

5. Your mental health is starting to decline.

Your mental health is one of the most important factors
of your life. It is just as important as your physical health.
In fact, it's been proven through scientific studies that if
you're struggling with your mental health, you can
become sick more often. Because your health is so
important, you have to make sure to keep your mental
health as healthy as possible. In order to do this, you
have to watch for any signs of feeling burned-out.
Unfortunately, once your mental health start to decline
you have felt burned-out for a while.

Once you start to notice yourself struggling with your
mental health, you can quickly run into other concerns,
such as anxiety and depression. You start to take less
care of yourself. For example, you might feel that you
don't have to eat healthy when you typically watch what
you eat. You might also stop exercising as you just don't
feel like it anymore. It is important to note that if you
start to feel this way, you should take a break from your
job as quickly as possible. Even taking a couple of days
or a week off can help you feel better about yourself and
set your motivation back on track.

Chapter 5: Learning the Art of

Swing Trading

The foundation of this chapter is to learn how to enter into the world of swing trading. However, before I get into actually learning about swing trading, it is important for you to remember a few basic points.

First, while swing trading is easy, you will probably find it a bit harder at the beginning. This should not make you feel that you cannot handle swing trading. However, it should help you realize that you will need to take time and continue to research and learn from others about the career of swing trading.

Second, even the most experienced swing traders make mistakes. There is no perfect guide when it comes to swing trading. You're going to make mistakes and will probably make more mistakes than some of the swing traders you know because you are just getting your start in the field. You should never let this deter you from becoming a successful swing trader. While some mistakes might make you lose more money than you thought, you should continue to learn from your mistakes as this will help you become more successful in the future. On top of this, you could become one of the next experienced swing traders who create their own website or book in hopes of helping beginners learn the art of swing trading.

Step 1: Start with Research

Throughout this book, you will read a lot about how research is important when you start getting into the field of swing trading. Of course, no matter what trading or investing you decide to do, you will always want to make sure to do your research and learn as much as you can about the topic. This is not only going to include website that you can find through a Google search, but also books from Amazon or your local library, and online classes. On top of this, you will want to join some online communities about swing trading, so you can get to know other swing traders and allow them to help you along your journey. It is important to note that swing traders aren't in competition with each other. Instead, when it comes to trading the person you are in competition with is yourself. When it comes to other swing traders, they want to do what they can to help you become successful. Therefore, online communities are a great resource when it comes to learning the trade.

Of course, before you start researching the topic, you will want to make sure you understand the basics of research. While you might have spent time in school researching for a few papers, this research will be more in-depth than other forms of research.

Tips to Help You Increase Your Research Skills

1. Start with Wikipedia – but don't use it as a source.

There is a lot of controversy around Wikipedia. There are people who believe that Wikipedia is one of the greatest websites to help you with your research and there are people who believe you shouldn't go near it if you are researching. However, when it comes to trading, Wikipedia is a great resource to start with. Not only can you get a general idea of what the topic is about, as people tend to easily explain things in Wikipedia, but you can also get a variety of websites from the list of citations at the end of the article.

In fact, no matter where you go to find your research, it is always a good idea to check some of the resources for that source. Not only will this help you confirm what the article is saying, but it can lead you to more educational or reliable sources.

2. Always make sure your source is reliable.

When it comes to research, a reliable source is the most important source you can find. There are many forms of reliable sources from government websites to people who are experts on the topic. Once you start researching and get an idea of what the topic is about, you will quickly be able to pick up the more reliable sources.

3. Look at your research like it is a puzzle.

One of the best ways to research is learn about one piece of your topic at a time. In a sense, you can look at your whole research topic as a puzzle you need to piece together. You start with one piece and then you move on to the next piece. You continue this process until your puzzle is completed. You can handle research the same way. You can first start by making a list of all the areas within your topic and then begin researching these sections one by one. As you research, you can make notes and write down ideas which can sometimes lead you in a better direction in your research.

4. Keep track of your sources.

One of the biggest mistakes that a lot of people make when they start researching is they don't keep track of their sources. There are a lot of ways that you can create a list of sources. For example, you can make a word document that holds the URL's from the internet sources you used. You could also make a bibliography which lists all the information about the sources.

5. You will need to be patient.

Unfortunately, you won't always find the information you need exactly when you want it. For example, there are times you might spend three hours researching the topic and barely find any information that you consider useful about your section. But, there will also be times where you research for a couple of hours and you find more resources that you thought you were going to.

6. Be consistent with your schedule and process.

Just as you will treat your new trading career as a profession, you want to do the same thing when it comes to researching for your new job. You will want to make sure you set time throughout your day for research. You will also want to make sure that you create a system and you keep using your system every time you work on your research. Doing this will be able to keep you more organized. On top of that, you will be able to understand what you are reading and learning better as you will have a clearer mind.

Step 2: Find a Broker

Because we already discussed the importance of not only finding a trusted broker but also knowing what your rights are, I am not going to go into that again. However, finding a broker is one of the early steps when you are getting into swing trading, therefore, it deserved a place on this list.

Once you find a broker, he or she will help you get started with setting up your account. On top of this, your broker will continue to help you with research, give you any advice you need, and answer any questions you have. This is another reason why it is important to find a broker early. It is always a good idea to have a like-minded individual that you can talk to about swing trading.

Step 3: Simulation Trading

After you start working with your broker, the next step is to look into simulation trading. While your broker should advise you to start your trading career with simulation trading, if he or she does not, then you should bring it up. With simulation trading, you will be able to get a real-time idea of what swing trading is like. The biggest plus of this is that you won't be losing any money if you make a mistake.

One of the biggest reasons you need to focus on simulation trading is because this will allow you to put your strategies and everything you have learned into practice. You will be able to find your strengths and weaknesses. On top of this, you can also make mistakes and find ways to learn from them, so you don't continue to make the mistakes in the future.

Another reason simulation trading is important is because it will allow you to start to get a sense of what trading is really like. No matter how much research you perform on swing trading, you will never truly be able to understand what the stock market and trading is actually like until you start to trade in real-time.

Step 4: Make Swing Trading Your New Career

Once you feel comfortable about trading. You can then start to look into working into trading with money. Once this happens, your days will start to become more like a career. Chances are you won't be working at swing trading full time during simulation trading, thought you could. However, once you start to get into trading with money, your days will become more consistent with the hours of the stock market.

A Swing Trader's Day

Pre-Trading Analysis

Your whole day at the stock market is going to be important, however, your morning pre-trading analysis can quickly make or break your career as a trader. You will want to take time before the stock market opens, which is 9:30 Eastern time, to get ready for the day, catch up on the news, see what change in the stock market overnight, and see how the foreign exchange market did. You can also use this time to see how your stocks are doing and scan the stock market to see what else catches your eye.

The Morning Stock Market

The New York Stock Exchange opens at 9:30 am, which means that you will have to adjust your time. For example, if you live in California, you will want to be ready for the stock market to open about 6:30 in the morning. This means that you will want to start your pre-trading analysis around 6:00 am or a little before, depending on how much time you take to analyze everything before the stock market opens.

It is important to note that for about the first half hour, the stock market is going to be very volatile. This means that there is going to be a lot of changes within the market and it will be unstable. Because of this, it is best to not make any move to sell or buy stocks. You want to let the market settle before you make any move. However, you can continue to scan the stock market to see if you can find your next interesting stock.

Once the volatile conditions slow down, usually around 10:10 in the morning, then you will start to see traders buying and selling. There will be a lot of day traders who are working on choosing their next best stock. On top of this, there will be a lot of other traders, including swing traders, who are thinking about buying and selling stocks.

Until around 10:30 am, you will find a lot of traders cashing out their trades. At this point, several of them will close out for the day. It is also around this time that you will start to see that stock market slowing down as people begin to get ready for lunch.

Lunch Time

When it comes to the stock market, the lunch time is between 11:00 am and 2:00 pm. During this time, the stock market is very quiet. If you are a full-time swing trader, this is around the time where you will not only grab lunch but also continue to work on research or just scan the stock market. You might also work on your afternoon plan. You won't be buying or selling very often during this time as there are not a lot of people taking part in the stock market.

The Afternoon Stock Market

Between 2:15 and 2:30 pm, you will start to see the stock market pick up again. This will happen because people are coming back from lunch and starting to get ready to close out the day. This means that the day traders will be quickly looking to sell all their stocks and swing traders will want to make sure that they are working on selling any stocks they need to at this point. As a swing trader, you might not sell and buy stocks every day. However, this doesn't mean that you won't be working. You will still want to take time to make sure that you keep up to date on the news, the information among the stock market, and your stocks.

In fact, the afternoon is a great time to start analyzing the stocks you have in your portfolio, especially if you have finished buying and selling any stocks you needed to for the day. You can spend this time looking at the trend lines and noticing what price your stocks sat at when the stock market opened, what the highest and lowest prices were. Furthermore, you can try to evaluate the stock and see if you can figure out the price the stock will close at. Doing this might help you gain more knowledge of how to analyze and establish a trend line, so you have an idea where it's heading to in the future.

About a half hour before the stock market closes, you will find that it becomes extremely busy again. This is the time where everyone is starting to close out for the day, which is exactly what you should be working on. If you have anything you have to close out, you will want to make sure to do this otherwise you can find that people will fill your orders without you realizing. When this happens, you can lose a lot of money. Therefore, if you have any orders that have not been filled, you must close them out before the end of the day.

After-Trading Analysis

Once the stock market officially closes about 4:00 pm Eastern time, you will be able to relax after a stressful day. On top of this, you will want to perform your after-trading analysis. This is when you take all the graphs you collected throughout the day from your trades, the current trades you hold, and start to analyze your graphs. While you are analyzing, you will want to pay attention to the trends and use the trends to follow a strategy to make sure you don't miss any details when it comes to analyzing your charts. In fact, many traders state that you should create a spreadsheet that lists everything you have to find during your after-trading analysis to make sure that you don't miss anything.

There are two basic ways that will help you record your after-trading analysis. One of these ways is to take a screenshot of all your charts and then makes notes in your charts. You will want to note the opening price, highest price, lowest price, and the closing price. On top of this, you will also want to make a note of any patterns you see in the trends, the conditions of the stock market, when you made the trade, why you decided to make the trade, and any distractions when you were making the trade.

Another way to help you keep up with your after-trading analysis is through having a trading journal. Similar to the charts, you will want to make sure to write down everything you can think of from your conditions at home to the conditions of the market. The reason why it is important to write down if you were distracted during a trade is because if you make a mistake, you can easily tell what might have caused you to make the mistake. For example, if you were making a trade and trying to feed your children at the same time, you might find that you should not complete both of these tasks at once. Instead, you will want to make sure that you have your time open when you need to take care of your children if you find them to be a distraction when it comes to trading.

One of the biggest reasons that you should keep a detailed analysis about your trading day, even if you just worked on research and didn't make a trade that day, is because you are able to analyze yourself as a trader. All experienced traders will tell you that everyone has a trading personality. Through how you handle the stock market, you will be able to find your strengths, weaknesses, and learn who you are as a trader. Of course, this can help you not only focus on building your strengths and turning your weaknesses into strengths, but it can also help you in finding target stocks for your investments or noticing when you are getting too emotional for the stock market.

Chapter 6: Trading Strategies

Like with any other version of trading, there are various strategies that you can use throughout your trading career. While most people like to stick to one or two strategies, which means they have to find financial instruments that work with their chosen strategies, other traders tend to go from one strategy to the next. However, as a beginner, it is best to realize that you should stick with one strategy as this will help you continue to learn about swing trading and how the stock market works in general. Of course, as you continue to build your trading knowledge and become more comfortable with swing trading, you can look into other strategies. While I cannot discuss all of the strategies in this chapter, I am discussing some of the most important and popular ones.

Trend Following

No matter what strategy you decide to use, you will need to make sure that you understand how to read charts and trend lines. You will use these tools in order to help guide you towards the best time to make your move to buy and sell a stock. When it comes to following a trend, there are a lot of details; such as what the opening price was, the highest price, the lowest price, and the closing price. You will analyze the trend over a period of time, how long depends on your personal preference. Through your analysis, you will start to notice a pattern in the trend line. This is the pattern that you will follow when you decide to take on a stock, see if your strategy will work for the stock, or what strategy to use.

The factors that you will look at when trend following are:

Price of the Stock

The price of the stock is one of the most important features that you will pay attention to. This doesn't just mean the price of the stock at that moment, such as what you would pay in order to purchase the stock. Even though the current price is the most important price, you will want to pay attention to all of the prices that you see for every day that you take into your analysis. For example, if you decide to look at the historical context of the last two months, you will look at about 60 days of stock pricing in order to help you find a trend. This means that you will look at the opening price for each of these days, the closing price, the highest price, and the lowest price. You will want to look at these prices in detail and in general. In a sense, this means that you will look at the larger image and the smaller pieces that make up the larger image.

Managing Your Money

Money management is thought to be one of the trickiest parts of trading. When it comes to managing your money, you want to make sure that you don't have too much money as it can give you a bigger loss. However, if you have too little money for the stock, then you aren't able to reach the full benefits when you make the trade. This is another time in swing trading when you want to find the best spot in order to make the trade.

One of the biggest tips to help you figure out how much money to put towards a stock is by evaluating the risks associated with the stock. You will be able to do this through any strategy that you will use and various other factors that are part of your trading plan.

Rules and Guidelines

One of the most important factors to remember when you are looking towards your trend line and thinking of making a trade. These rules are not only the guidelines that you will receive as you start to learn the swing trading technique, they are also the rules that you will set for yourself. For example, if you decide that your stop-loss price is going to be $10.00 lower than the price you bought the stock from, you will want to make sure that you follow this guideline.

One of the biggest reasons you need to make sure that you are following your guidelines is because the more consistent you are with your trading, the more likely you are to become successful. Furthermore, you will want to make sure that you follow the guidelines as they will help you to think systematically when it comes to making decisions. While you might find yourself turning back to your trading plan and guidelines consistently as a beginner, the more you follow the same procedures, the more you will focus on them as a way in making sure you are following the steps instead of needing them more for direct reference on where to go and what to do next. In a sense, trading will start to become more natural to you, which is a great strength when you are analyzing trend lines.

Diversity

Diversity is one of the more popular controversies when it comes to trading. While some traders feel you need to have great diversity, which is a variety of stocks, in your portfolio others feel that this isn't as important. In reality, the more serious you want to be with your trading, the more you will focus on diversity. However, this isn't always true when it comes to investors. But, as stated before, investing and trading are two different career paths in the stock market.

You can look at diversity as what is the right feature for you. You might find that you don't need to have a large diversity because you are a part-time swing trader or you have a specific target that you focus on. However, you might also find that the more diversity you have, the better-rounded you feel as a trader. You might find that diversity is helping you learn more about investing in general.

Always Note the Risk

Another important factor to pay attention to when you are looking into trend following is how much risk is involved if you decide to take on the financial instrument you are looking at. When you are looking at the risk, you always have to pay attention to your guidelines and your trading plan. These two factors will help you decide if you should take on the stock due to the risk it carries or not. It is important to remember you need to stick to the risk level you are comfortable with. Even if you think that this stock could give you good rewards, this doesn't mean that you should agree to take on the financial instrument if you are uncomfortable with the risk.

This also doesn't mean that you can't increase your risk level as time goes on. You just want to make sure that you build your confidence and comfort level with risk as your risk grows. Furthermore, as you get more knowledgeable with swing trading, it might be a good thing to slowly increase your risk when it comes to taking on stocks. It's always good to grow in many directions as a trader, including with risk.

Trend following tends to be one of the most popular techniques when it comes to trading because it has a high success rate, providing you understand where the trend line is heading. Of course, you should always remember that the stock market can take drastic turns and no one can truly predict the future. This means, even if you analyze the trend lines to the best degree, you will still have some risk involved as the trend line could differ a bit from what you originally thought.

Using Options as a Strategy

We have already discussed what options are; however, one factor I did not discuss is how options are usually seen as a strategy when it comes to trading. Because you are able to set up an agreement which gives you the option to buy or sell the stock later, you are technically strategizing the right time to take the next step in the future.

One of the biggest ways to do this is through analyzing the various charts that you see for your stock. In fact, you will focus a lot on technical analysis, which is something I will discuss later. You will focus on the historical charts of the stock as this will give you a time-frame for when you will want to take the next step.

Options are known to be a great strategy if you are looking for leverage, which is when you increase a return on a trade through borrowed money. It is important that you need to make sure you will only use this strategy if it will help you to receive more of a profit. In fact, this is one of the most important factors of choosing a strategy. You have to make sure that it is going to help you gain a profit and decrease your risks.

Short Interest

Many experienced traders state that beginners should not take part in the short interest strategy as it tends to be more of a guessing game than other strategies. When you focus on the short interest strategy, you will compare the number of short shares to the number of floating shares.

This is a great strategy to learn as a swing trader because it can show when the stock market is about to go into bearish conditions, which means that the stock prices will start to go down. Furthermore, short interest can also warn you about short squeezing.

Pay Attention to the Float

One of the best ways that you can tell if a trade is going to help you is through a technique known as float. Basically, a float is the total number of shares that a trader will find in public sharing. This can become very helpful because, if you have the right size of float, you can see higher profits.

However, this is also the trick when it comes to the float strategy. There tends to be a fine line between having a massive float and having a float that will give you the best profits. The reason why a massive float, which would be too many shares, can cause you to lose capital instead of increasing your profits is because if you have a huge float, the price won't move as quickly. However, if you have a smaller amount of shares in your float, then you will find that the price moves a bit higher, of course this gives you a larger profit. With this said, you also don't want to have too little shares in your float. If this happens, then you won't be able to make much of a profit either as this can stop your float from increasing in price.

Breakout and Breakdown Strategies

When you focus on the breakout strategy, you are looking at the history of your stock's trend line in a microscopic fashion. What I mean by this is you will be focusing on what the trend has done over the past few days. When you are looking at the trend line, you will see every time the price has gone up and down. Stock prices are almost constantly changing throughout the day, which is what the trend line shows. Every now and then, you will notice in the trend line that you have a several high points and several low points. These high points indicated the highest prices of the stock and the lowest points show the lowest prices.

The biggest difference between the breakout strategy compared to the breakdown strategy is the condition of the market. If you notice that the stock has been going on an upward trend for a while, you will use the breakout strategy. However, if you notice that the trend shows the price has been decreasing over time, you will use the breakdown strategy.

Of course, for both strategies, there is that specific spot you need to try in order to gain your best profit. The best spot to make your next move will depend on the pattern of the trend.

News Playing

As you know by now, one of the most important parts of your day is your pre-trading portion. This is one of the first things you will do once you start your day. You will want to do this before you start trading; however, you will probably be checking out the stock market so you can see the changes in your stocks and any target stocks that you are watching.

However, one of the most important parts of this part of the day is reading the news that happened over night. This is important because you need to know what news is going to affect what stock, especially if you own the stock. You should always make note that any type of news can affect the pricing of financial instruments. For example, if you read that a company donated a large amount of money towards a nonprofit organization, people might be more likely to invest in that stock. However, if you read any negative news about a company, you will find the stock price going down because people are selling their shares.

But, you need to remember the trick of keeping your emotions out of the stock market. While News Playing is a strategy which is used all across the board when it comes to the stock market, for example all traders and investors use this strategy, it is important to remember that you should never make a decision to sell or take on a stock because of your emotions. I won't go much more into this because I discuss how your emotions can be a risk factor in the stock market in another chapter, but it is also a big part of News Playing that you have to look out for.

You always want to make sure that you think logically when you are making a decision to buy or sell a stock. Even if you find you hold a stock where the price is dropping due to negative news, you want to make sure you continue to follow your trading plan instead of going on your emotions. Therefore, you should only focus on selling the stock if the price drops to your stop-loss price. You also should not hold on to a stock for longer than you originally planned, even if they are the center of a positive news story. While you can be a little flexible when the price continues to rise, at least in swing trading, you don't want to hold on to the stock for longer than a swing trader should. You always have to keep the time-frame in mind.

Chapter 7: The Art of Selling

Short

One of the biggest pieces of advice you will hear from other traders is that you have to buy low and sell high if you want to make the best profit. This makes complete sense. Think about how retail markets work. Stores will often buy their stock at a lower price than what they sell them for. For example, the store owners might be able to purchase a notebook for $1.00 a piece, but when they put the notebook out on their shelves, they will most likely raise the price, which means you could be buying the notebooks for $1.50, which gives the store a .50 cent profit on each notebook they sell.

You want to think the same when you are trading stocks. You want to make sure that when you complete your trading plan for that particular stock that you set a stop-loss price as this will tell you how low you are willing to go. For example, if you decide that you don't want less than a dollar loss on a stock, you will set your stop-loss price at a dollar less than you paid for the stock. Of course, you hope that you will make a profit, which means that you will sell the stock at a higher price than what you paid for.

I have already discussed the difference between bull market and bear markets; however, to give you a bit of a review, a bull market occurs when the stock market is doing well and prices are rising. A bear market occurs when the stock market prices are dropping. So, when it comes to a bear market, you might ask why people trade as there isn't a way for them to make a profit. However, there is a way that traders can continue to make a profit when the stock market is seeing low numbers and this is through a technique called short selling.

How Short Selling Works

Unless you become a day trader, most traders will believe that they will hold on to their stock for a good period of time. Of course, when it comes to swing trading, you won't – or shouldn't – hold on to a stock for longer than a couple of months. With that stated, there are many beginning traders who feel that they are going to start trading and hold the stock for as long as possible as this will give them their best profit. If this is what you are thinking, you are looking more towards investing than trading.

The basic definition of short selling is when a trader takes on stock knowing that he or she is going to sell the stock after it has fallen in value. Of course, this is something that you are typically told not to do. However, there are many people who have used this position during bear markets and have found that it can be profitable. But, you are probably wondering how, if the price has lowered, the trader makes a profit from short selling. The truth of this trick is simple – the trader never actually takes ownership of the stock. Now your next question might be how a trader can sell a stock, and receive a profit, when he or she doesn't even own the stock. To look at this in a more basic way, let's look at it in two parts.

First, you have the part where the trader borrows the stock. This is usually done through a loan, which is similar to borrowing money from the bank. This means that the trader fully intends to buy the stock he sold back, which brings us to the second point. Because the stock prices continue to decline, the trader knows that he or she will be buying back the stock at a lower price than what they sold it for. Once they rebuy the stock, they send it back to the original owner, which closes out the loan, and the trader was able to make a bit of profit.

In order to start short selling, you will open a margin account through your broker. This account will use your profits in your account as collateral, just as a car is used as collateral for a vehicle loan. This means that if you are unable to repay your broker back in any way, your broker still receives the money as he or she can take it right out of your account. Furthermore, you need to note that you must be able to follow the 2:1 ratio when it comes to short selling. This means that your account must have at least 50% of what you are asking to borrow. For example, if you are asking to borrow $10,000 then you will have to have $5,000 in your account.

You need to be able to sell the stock to the first willing buyer. There isn't a huge time-frame for short selling. In fact, it tends to happen very quickly. Then, once the stock has sold, you have to go to the open market with that money and find a lower price for that stock. As you are doing this, it is important to remember that you have to buy back as many shares as you borrowed. Once you decide on your stocks, you will then inform your broker, who will make the transaction through your margin account. From there, your broker will receive his or her funds and you will receive the remaining profit.

The Risks of Short Selling

Of course, there are a lot of risk when it comes to short selling. The biggest risk is that you can never really tell the future. No matter how much you analyze charts or the general stock market conditions, such as if it's a bull or bear market, you will never be able to officially tell what a stock or the market is going to do. Because of this, one of your biggest risks is that you will have to buy back the stock at a higher price than what you sold it as. If this happens, you will take a loss instead of make the profit.

Another great risk when short selling is that you can get yourself into debt. Think of this – if you are unable to make a profit and you borrowed $20,000, this means you only have about $10,000 in your account. Therefore, not only will your broker take all the money in your account, but you still have to pay back the remaining $10,000.

Short selling is very strategic which can be risky, especially for a beginner. Short selling can seem like a very strange way to do things during an economic downturn. In fact, many beginners often question if short selling is even legal. Which it is, short selling is completely legal and is known to be a popular practice when the stock market is in bull conditions. However, because of its strategy and its risks, it can also be confusing for a beginner, even though you will be working with your broker.

Therefore, like with any other strategy, you want to make sure that you fully understand everything there is about short selling from the process to its risks before you decide to take on this technique during poor stock market conditions. While short selling occurs in a way that is meant to protect the trader's account, you also want to make sure that you understand that you can still bring yourself into debt if the process doesn't work as well as it should. You will also want to make sure that you go through the same trading plan, research, and following all your rules and guidelines before you decide to short sell. Understanding exactly what the stock market and the stock is doing will help limit your chance of a huge loss and, potentially, bringing yourself into debt.

Chapter 8: Tips for Beginners

Below are a variety of tips that you can carry with you into your new swing trading career. These tips are taken from experienced traders who want to give you the best advice that they can, so you can begin your new job with a positive mindset and feel ready to take on the swing trading world.

Learn from Your Mistakes and Move On

Successful traders learn several lessons early on in their career. One of these is mistakes are going to happen and when they do, you have to learn from it and move on. You cannot continue to hang on to the mistake you made as this won't help you psychologically. It is important as a trader to note that you should always be in the right frame of mind. When you start to dwell on your mistakes, then you are more likely to become emotional. This can allow your emotions to make decisions instead of thinking logically.

Even if you make a mistake that you read about on this list. This happens. You don't want to put too much stress on this mistake. Instead, you want to realize that you made the mistake, figure out what you can do so you are less likely to make the mistake in the future, and then move on.

Stay in the Right Mindset

Every successful swing trader knows that one of the most important pieces of the career is having the right mindset. The basis of this mindset is to believe that when you are confident in your abilities and you believe that you can become a successful swing trader, you will become a successful trader. There are a lot of parts to developing this mindset and it can take time, especially if you lack patience, confidence, and don't believe that you will be successful.

No matter where your mindset sits at this point, it will take time to develop the best mindset. When you work on creating this mindset, you want to focus on specific factors that will help boost your confidence. In return, you will start to believe in your abilities, start to feel that you will be successful, and then be able to hold this mindset throughout your career. It is important to note that in order to keep this mindset, you do have to remember that mistakes happen and not to take them too personally. As I stated before, learn from the mistakes and move on.

To help you develop and stay in the right mindset, you will want to follow a variety of techniques that I discuss throughout this book. For example, you want to follow your trading plan, remain flexible, realize mistakes happen, follow your schedule, keep your emotions in check, establish and evaluate your goals, and find the techniques and strategies that work for you.

Be Flexible

Many people get into the swing trading business with the belief that they have to follow the rules and guidelines exactly as they are written. On top of this, they believe that they have to make sure to follow their own rules exactly as they were created. In reality, when you become inflexible to the world of swing trading, including the rules, then you will start to feel stressed. This stress can put you in the wrong mindset for trading. For example, it can make you feel that you are not capable of becoming a successful trader.

While you want to follow the rules and guidelines, you should also remain flexible. First, you want to remember that life happens. Sometimes we plan to sit down to work but we have to go pick up a sick child from school or have a family emergency. When this happens, we might not be able to complete the financial instruments that we took on. This means that you will either keep them in your portfolio and take any loss or hope for a gain or you can trade them and close out for the day. When you are flexible, you will realize that this situation will be fine, and you won't dwell on the fact that you couldn't complete the job as you should have.

Remaining flexible will also help when you find yourself with unrealistic expectations, which is a common mistake among traders. On top of this, it will help you realize that mistakes happen and you shouldn't put too much emphasis on them.

Remember the Research

Learning is a common theme as a trader. It doesn't matter what type of trading you find yourself taking on, you will always want to make sure that you learn as much as you can before you start your career and continue to learn. There are a variety of ways that you can focus on research and learning with swing trading. For example, reading this book is one way that you are researching and learning. You can continue to find other books that will help you along your swing trading journey. In fact, there are a variety of books on the topic that can help you. Some of these books I used for my research in this book while others I found along the way and thought I would include them in the following list.

Swing Trading: A Step By Step Guide To Trade Stocks, Forex And Options For Big Profits by Steve Arnold received publication in 2019 and is one of the newest books on the topic. This is a great book if you are interested in certain types of trading.

How To Swing Trade: A Beginner's Guide to Trading Tools, Money Management, Rules, Routines and Strategies of a Swing

Trader by Brian Pezim and Andrew Aziz received publication in 2018. This is one of the most comprehensive books on the market about swing trading.

Swing Trading: A Beginner's Guide to Highly Profitable Swing Trades - Proven Strategies, Trading Tools, Rules, and Money Management by Mark Lowe. This book is another one of the newest books on the market and is a great comprehensive beginner's book.

Swing trading: A guide for beginners, the best strategies for making profits in trading, forex, passive income, how to make money online in a few simple steps by Andrew J. Wolf received publication in 2019.

Join an Online Community

Another great way to learn about swing trading and meet other traders is to join an online community. There are several websites that are comprised of forums run by some of the most experienced swing traders today. These forums are extremely beneficial to any trader for a variety of reasons. First, beginners can go join the community and receive more tips, trading lessons, and other information that will help them become successful. Second, this is often a location where beginners meet their trading mentor. Third, this is a place where traders can go to not only get the most up-to-date information on the profession but also get to know people who are like them. It is always important to feel that you are not alone, especially when find yourself struggling with a part of trading. There will be hundreds, if not thousands, of people who will be interested in helping you.

Below are a few swing trading online communities that you can check out. Of course, it never hurts to check out as many communities as you can find to see which one is the best fit for you. You can do this by scanning the website to see what information is available to you, by price (unfortunately, not all the online communities are free), or by joining and figuring out over time which communities you like the most. You never know who you will meet along your journey.

The Trading Heroes Blog

This is a swing trading & currency trading education online community. This blog started in 2016 and focuses on forex education and trading. Over the last few years, this blog has grown to become one of the top swing trading blogs online. The owner publishes about one post per month; however, he is often found on the blog and is willing to help other swing traders with advice.

Elite Swing Trading

This is one of the most in-depth swing trading websites available. The site is run by Jason Bond Picks and gives not only a place where other traders can converse but also a newsletter with helpful information and tips for everyone involved in the swing trading community.

Morpheus Trading Group

This is an online community that focuses on how to trade stocks. This community started around 2002 and has steadily grown to become one of the most helpful communities online. You will receive about one post per month which will give you all types of helpful information to help you through your swing trading journey.

Ratgebergeld

If you want to find a community that gives you a little more than just one post every month, you can check out Ratgebergeld. This is a site that focuses on both swing trading and day trading. You will receive about two posts a week which focus on the most up-to-date information and a live chat. There are generally several experienced traders who are a part of this chat and are ready to help you with any problems you might be having in the moment.

Make Education a Top Priority

One of the most important factors when it comes to trading is your education. Most traders don't often take time to truly focus on their education before they start trading, which can make their journey more challenging at first. Sometimes they decide they can't afford the classes, while other times they feel that they will be able to learn better by actually performing the trades. Though both of these reasons are realistic, it is important that you do not skip the education focus. Of course, any research you complete will be part of this focus. However, there are also online classes that you can join to help you get the best handle on swing trading from the start.

Professional Swing Trading A-Z

Professional Swing Trading A-Z is one of the top trading courses which heavily discusses this topic for beginners. While you do need to pay, they will often have sale prices for their classes. Not only will you learn about the basics of swing trading but you will also get into technical analysis, fundamental analysis, various techniques and strategies, and learn how to perform a trade. On top of all this, the instructor is always available to help people who are ready or have already started their own account. Furthermore, you will learn about risk management and receive nearly 14 hours of video lessons. Unlike some courses, you don't need to have any type of previous knowledge about swing trading to take this class. In fact, you could sign up today!

Guide to Stock Trading with Candlestick and Technical Analysis

This is another course that is specifically meant for beginners who are interested in different forms of trading that focuses on stocks, such as swing trading. While you will get basic information, the majority of this class focuses on technical analysis and how to read and handle a candlestick chart. The course is run by Luca Moschini of Sharper Trade and has received high praise for being one of the best courses for the past few years. While the class is about $60, there are often sale prices that you can take advantage of.

Day Trading and Swing Trading Systems for Stocks and Options

If you have a little experience with swing trading, then you might want to check out this course. You will need some experience before you sign up for the day trading and swing trading system for stocks and options course. It is known as an intermediate course but it is very comprehensive with the topics the class covers. Udemy runs this course, in fact Udemy runs most of the courses mentioned in this section. After you pay $100 to register for the course, you will receive access to various downloadable information and hours of video lessons.

Chapter 9: Common Mistakes Beginners Make

Whether you are a beginner or expert swing trader, you will find yourself making mistakes. However, mistakes are more commonly made when you are a beginner. Before I go any further I want to let you know that this doesn't meant that you should think twice about making swing trading your new career. Mistakes are going to happen, and no one knows this better than experts. Therefore, many of them have shared their mistakes with the hope that beginners will remember the mistakes and, therefore, do what they can to avoid them.

You Have Unrealistic Expectations

There are many traders who come into the stock market world with a lot of unrealistic expectations. There are several reasons for this. For example, some might believe that trading is a career which will quickly make them rich while other people might believe that it is an easy work-from-home type job. While you can work from home when you become a swing trader, the job is not as easy as many people believe. In fact, it can be a very stressful job with a lot of factors involved from research to your post-trading analysis at the end of your work day.

In fact, when people have unrealistic expectations, it can cause a lot of problems. These problems have led many beginners to believe that they could not become a successful trader. While they didn't all quit their new career, many did. It is important to remember that you should never give up on your trading career too quickly, even if you feel that you barely know anything about trading or you realize that trading is different than what you initially thought. You should continue to research and learn about swing trading as you might like it once you get through the first few months.

The reason I am telling you that it is important to try to get through the first few months of trading is because most traders will tell you that there were many times they thought of quitting during this time. Learning trading is not an easy task. It takes a lot of dedication, patience, time, and can become very stressful at times. However, if you are truly invested in becoming a trader, you will be able to make it through these first few months. Even though you will come to realize that you had several unrealistic expectations and obstacles to go through, you were able to make it by holding on to your dedication for your new career.

If you find yourself having unrealistic expectations it is important to realize there is nothing wrong with this. In fact, you should be proud that you have noted your unrealistic expectations and can now work to change them into more realistic expectations. Furthermore, if you think about previous careers you have held, you have probably gone into your new job with unrealistic expectations. This is common when it comes to people starting new positions. One of the biggest reasons for this is because people often believe that they can take on more than they actually can when they receive a new job or even a promotion. There is always a settlement period where people start to see the reality of their new positions. During this time, they are not only learning what they can do but also what they need to work a little more on.

You Don't Follow Your Pre-Trading Analysis

I have already mentioned how important following your pre-trading analysis is. However, there are many people who start to feel that they don't need to take the time to do this for various reasons. Sometimes the reason is as simple as people are running late and just don't want to take the time when the stock market is opening. Of course, other reasons tend to follow more in the mindset that they understand how trading works and, therefore, don't need to take part in these activities anymore.

While you might feel that there is a lot of research to complete as you get your day started, you still need to make sure to take the time to check out the information. You need to make sure that you completely understand what is going on in the stock market world from the news to the changes that occurred overnight.

Of course, there have been many traders who admitted to not always following through with their pre-trading analysis. They have stated that on these days they noted they didn't perform as well. For example, they made more mistakes because they weren't briefed on the changes that the stock market made overnight or the news about a company that they held a share for. They also admitted that it made them feel like they were out of the loop in general. The stock market is constantly changing, which means you need to keep up with these changes and change with the market. If you don't take the time to do this, you will quickly fall behind.

You Don't Follow Through with Your Post-Trading Analysis

You can also quickly fall behind in the stock market world if you don't complete your post-trading analysis after the stock market closes every day. This is a very important part of your day because it will help you become a successful trader. It is important to remember that you will not become successful overnight. In fact, it takes traders years to reach the level of success that they imagine themselves reaching. This is because it takes a lot of time and practice with the stock market to not only understand it but learn all the details and tricks of the trade.

Because I discussed your post-trading analysis earlier, I am not going to spend too much more time explaining what it is. However, you should note that throughout your analysis, you need to remember to write as much down as possible. This is very important and could also be something that you change over time. For example, you might start recording the times that you made the trades during the day. However, as you continue to analyze your post-trades over the last few months, you find out that writing down the time isn't doing anything to help you grow. In fact, you might start to see this as a worthless number. If you reach this point, you have two options. First, you can continue to write down the time because you might need this information one day. Second, you could decide to stop writing the time down. One thing to remember if you start to think about skipping the time is that you never know when you are going to need certain information in the future. While a statistic might not be helpful today, it could be helpful in a couple months.

This is one of those times where you have to remember that you are still learning all the details about swing trading. Even if you are writing down information after working as a swing trader for six months and begin to believe some of the statistics are meaningless, you should still continue to write them down. First, it is always important to remain consistent as a trader. Second, because you are learning every day, you might come across a more experienced swing trader or other information that will explain to you why this meaningless statistic is actually meaningful. When this happens, you will be grateful that you continued to write down the numbers instead of ignoring them.

You are Not Consistent

Now that I have mentioned consistency, it seems to be a good time to mention that inconsistency seems to be a common mistake that beginner traders make. Of course, there can be a variety of reasons for this from they don't remember all the steps they have to follow to they start to feel more confident in their abilities. While feeling confident is good, this shouldn't mean that you start to take your job less seriously or feel that you can skip some steps because you believe you have a better hold of what swing trading is.

You want to create a theme in your swing trading career that helps you remain consistent. Because swing trading can become a stressful career, consistency will help you maintain a healthy mental balance. Furthermore, you will be more likely to remember what you need to do and when. Of course, you will always have a trading plan or business plan to help you with these steps, it is important that you know these steps as well as you know the meaning of swing trading.

Another reason remaining consistent can help is through giving you a healthier professional and personal life balance. While some people feel that they can connect the two, more people feel that they need to create a balance in order to remain happy and content in the personal and business life. Being consistent in your job can help with this because you are more likely to follow the hours that you decide to use for your work day. For example, if you are a full-time swing trader in New York City. You might work from about 9:00 am to around 4:30 pm Monday through Friday. Even if you work at home, you want to keep these hours because this will help tell you that the hours outside of this time are reserved for your personal life.

You Don't Pay Attention to Your Mental Health

Your mental health is just as important as your physical health. However, people tend to pay less attention to their mental health. For example, when you are feeling depressed you don't often take the day off in order to get better like you would if you had a bad cold or the flu.

While there are several reasons to why people tend to push their mental health aside, it is something that you need to make sure you take care of. Not only is this important for everyone, but it is important for a swing trader due to many reasons.

First, swing traders need to remain in the right mindset. Because I have discussed the right mindset previously, I am not going to go too much into that. However, I will take time to note that your mental health heavily depends on being able to reach the right mindset. For example, if you are trying to reach the right mindset, you need to be able to reach a level of confidence in yourself. If you are constantly putting yourself down for every mistake you make or you become overly critical of yourself, you will not be able to reach this right mindset. Therefore, your mental health and your right mindset to become a successful swing trader go hand in hand.

Other than making you believe that you can become a successful day trader, being mentally healthy can also help you keep from being stressed. It is important to make sure that you don't become too stressed as a trader because this can lead you into a variety of other issues from lack of confidence to making more mistakes. On top of that, becoming too stressed can cause you to make decisions based on an emotion. Stress is an emotion which often brings forth other emotions. As stated before, you want to make sure that you do not make decisions based on your emotions because you will be more likely to make a mistake or jump too quickly when you see the price of a stock fall.

Chapter 10: The 11 Commandments of Swing Trading

Some of the most experienced swing traders of 2019 like to focus on what has become known as the 11 commandments of swing trading. Popular trader, Melvin Pasternak, developed this list and discusses it after his trading classes.

1. Make Sure to Have Long Strengths and Short Weaknesses

There are two periods that you should be looking for when you are taking on a trade. The first period is known as bull and the second period is known as bear. You need to be able to identify these periods when you get into the market because this will let you know what the market conditions are like for that time.

When you look at the bull market condition, you are looking at an increasing market. The stock trends are on an upward trend, which they have been on for a good period of time. This proves that the levels of the economy are high and you should spend your time looking for longer trades.

When the market's condition is focused on bearishness, this means that the stocks are on a downward trend. The prices of stocks are dropping and many traders believe that this is the spiral that they will see in some stocks for a period of time. Bear conditions happen when the economy isn't doing very well. This is normally during points of economic recession and when unemployment is high. When you notice the bear conditions, you will want to focus on short trades as this will limit your risk of loss, especially if the downward trend continues.

2. The Overall Direction of the Market and Your Trade Should be Aligned

This is one reason research is important. You not only want to research when you are starting your swing trade profession, but you also want to continue your research. In fact, every day that you sit down in front of your desk, is a day that you will be doing research. One of these reasons is because you have to make sure to research and analyze every stock. This will help you determine whether you should purchase the stock or not.

When you are focusing on your research for a particular stock, one of the main focuses should be does the stock match the overall direction of the market? When it comes to the stock market, you will find that it's either on an upward or downward spiral. You will want to match your trade with this direction.

3. Always Look at the Long-Term Charts

One of the biggest mistakes that beginner traders often make is that they will only focus on the short-term charts when they are looking into a stock. Many experienced traders feel that this is the wrong course of action as you should have a better idea of what the trend of the stock has done over at least a six-month period. Of course, you can always go longer than six months.

You should start with the chart that will give you a couple of weeks. From there, you will want to make sure you go over the chart and notice every single detail. There is nothing that you should miss during the analysis of your chart. After you have looked at the first couple of weeks, then you can dive more into a long-term chart, such as the six-month chart. Again, follow the same microscopic process you did with the previous chart. Do your best not to miss anything. In fact, some traders will often create an excel spreadsheet where they can list everything they have to view in the chart and even write down information. This is a great piece of advice for any beginner.

4. Do Your Best Not to Enter Near the End of the Trade

Once you start to get into the stock market, you will notice a trend when it comes to traders. You will find that the stock market is busy within the first hour because there are so many traders who are buying new stocks for the day. You will then notice that the stock market begins to get quiet around the 11:00 hour because people are either holding on to their stocks or closed out for the day. However, about the last hour, which starts around 3:00 pm, you will notice the stock market picks up again as people, especially day traders, sell all their stocks and close out.

As a swing trader, you might not buy and sell stocks every day. Unlike day traders, you can hold your stocks for a few days to about a week or two. However, there are a few traders that are not allowed to do this as it would cause them too much loss.

Another reason people enter into trades earlier rather than later is because this can give you the most profit, especially if you find a stock that is hitting an upward trend. On top of this, you will have less risk to worry about if you enter a trade early. Doing your best to cut down on risk is always something traders focus on, even if they don't mind taking risks.

5. Track a Consistent Group of Stocks

Just like every trader is different, every stock is different. This is why it is important to not focus on jumping from one stock to the next. Instead, as you are learning the tricks and strategies of swing trading, you will want to start getting an idea of what kind of stocks you like. Every stock has its own personality and once you catch on to that specific personality, trading will become easier if you stick to groups of stocks that are similar.

One reason for this is because you will most likely be able to use the same strategy for all of your stocks. This can help you when it comes to learning techniques and strategies. It is easier to stick to one strategy because there are so many tiny details about swing trading you need to remember, the human brain can only hold so much information.

Another reason for this is because this allows you to be able to manage a certain amount of stocks consistently. If you are a full-time swing trader, you will find this system will give you less stress, keep your focus, and increase confidence in your abilities. Of course, all this will help you keep your right state of mind as a trader.

6. Always Have a Clear Plan

Whenever you enter a trade, you will want to make sure that you have a clear plan of action. This plan will most likely be your trading plan; however, this is known to change from time to time as traders start to learn and grow with their profession. While this is great as it means you are becoming a more successful trader, you will also want to make sure that you continue to update and adjust your plan as you need to.

Before you enter any trade, it is best to go through your plan and make sure that it will work with that stock. If you find it won't, then you will need to either adjust your trading plan or choose a stock that will fit your trading plan better.

You will want to make sure that everything is including in this plan from your entry to your exit. You will want to make sure that you have all the key points and details down. On top of this, you will also want to make sure that you have a stop-loss strategy in place so you can quickly let go of that stock through a trade and walk away from losing a large amount of money. Remember, when you decide the stop-loss strategy is the best course of action, it will happen quickly. In fact, trading is a very faced-paced business, which is another reason making sure you always have a clear plan of action is a commandment.

7. Always Integrate Fundamentals into Your Technical Analysis

While I will discuss technical analysis later in this book, one of the 11 commandments of swing trading is to make sure that you integrate fundamentals into your analysis. If you have looked into day trading, you will know a bit about fundamentals and more about technical analysis. However, when it comes to swing trading, fundamentals becomes just as important as technical analysis. The main reason for this is because you hold your stocks longer than a few minutes to a few hours.

8. Make Sure to Master the Psychological side of Swing Trading

As you will see later in this book, there is a lot of psychology that goes into swing trading. In fact, psychology goes into any type of trading, but it is more crucial when it comes to swing traders. While part of this is about keeping the right mindset, the other part comes from the overall experience of swing trading. There are a lot of factors, such as making mistakes, learning, and losing that can affect your psyche throughout your day. For example, if you take a loss you might find that you feel like a failure after you have closed out your day. This can affect your personal life as well as your working life. It is extremely important to make sure that you have a healthy frame of mind and not just the right mindset when you are a trader.

9. Try Putting the Odds in Your Favor

Sometimes you will look at a trade and wonder if you will be able to make a profit on it. This is why it is important to use technical analysis with every trade. However, even if you feel that you might not be able to make a profit, this doesn't mean that you walk away from the trade. In fact, you can take this time to work on putting the odds in your favor. While this means you might end up risking a profit, trading is always full of risks. In fact, you will never be able to fully eliminate risks. Therefore, there are times where you have to take the leap and use certain techniques in order to try to work the trade into your favor.

One way to do this is by having a target price, which should always be a part of your target plan. This price will tell you when you should quickly turn to sell or trade the stock and when you should hold on to it for a bit longer. No matter what the market conditions are, you always want to stick to your target price. Therefore, you want to make sure that you complete your technical analysis to the best of your abilities before you go forward with your trading plan.

Furthermore, it is important to not only assess the chart once but also to reassess the chart. This means that you don't just analyze the chart before you take on the trade as you will continue to look at the chart and see what the stock's trend is doing in real-time. This means that you will notice the stock price increase and decreasing throughout the time you are analyzing.

10. Trade in Harmony with the Trend Time Frames

When it comes to the stock market, there are three types of trend time frames. The longest time frame is a year. The intermediate time frame is about three months. The shortest time frame is less than a month. When you are a swing trader, you will typically focus on the intermediate and short-term time frames. However, there are traders who have stated that they have looked at trends as far back as six months. Typically, swing traders don't have to focus on the longer time frame because they are considered to be short-term traders. At the same time, swing traders need to do more than just look at the short-term trend lines.

In fact, many expert swing traders will tell beginners that if they only focus on the short-term time frame, they are more likely to make mistakes. While you can always get a good sense of what the stock is doing with the short-term time frame, this can also limit you. The stock market is a very unpredictable place. This means that the further you look back, the better your idea will be about the type of trend that goes with the stock. The key is to heavily focus on the short-term trends and then do an analysis of the intermediate trends.

11. Make Sure to Use Multiple Indicators and Not Create Isolation

Sometimes traders will often feel that they only need to use one tool to give them an idea of what stock will give them a profitable trade and what stock won't. You should never do this. You always want to make sure that you use multiple tools and that these tools give you consistent results. For example, you might use a strategy, candlestick chart, volume, and other tools in order to find out that your trade will be profitable.

One of the reasons this is important is because it helps you limit your risks. The more tools you have that give you consistent results, the more likely you are to be able to make a profit.

Chapter 11: Fundamental Analysis

When you are trying to find the best stock to take on, you want to focus on different analyses which will help you make an informed decision. One of these types of analysis is fundamental analysis. The other one is known as technical analysis, which I will cover in the next chapter. Because each of these types are extremely important, I wanted to discuss them in detail, so I decided they should have their own chapters.

Fundamental analysis is performed when you are doing general research on a company. For example, if you are interested in purchasing Amazon stock, you will start to look into the company. You might start with the company's history to get a sense of the overall growth of the entity itself. You might decide that looking over the last few years will give you enough history to help you make an informed decision. While how much research you do is more of your personal preference and how serious you take your career as a trader, I believe that the more information you have on a company, the better chance you have of becoming successful.

Fundamental Variables

There are going to be several questions that come to your mind immediately as you start to perform research on a company. For example, you might ask yourself how long the company has been successful. You might ask yourself if this is a company you believe will give you a good profit or if this company has a history of getting traders high returns. Whatever questions you ask yourself, you need to realize that you have to do more than just ask the basic questions. In fact, you have to make sure you take time to look at the fundamental variables.

Positive Earnings Adjustment

In the trading world, there are people who are known as market analysts. These are people who will often analyze how well companies are doing and then give the companies a review or a forecast, which allows other people to notice where the company is sitting. Market reviewers are typically known as cautious people and don't tend to believe that companies will pass their forecast. However, this does happen and when it does, it brings us into positive earnings adjustment.

Basically, this states that we need to look for stocks which have surprised the market analysts. This is because if companies pass their forecast, they will continue to succeed. Therefore, they become known as one of the best companies to gain a profit from, which is always a great thing for a trader to know. However, you will still want to make sure that you do your deep analysis before making any moves on a stock.

Positive Earning Revision

This is the process that market analysts go through when they are evaluating how well a company is doing so they can give them a forecast. As stated above, these analysts are cautious and very careful to note where they think the company is going. Therefore, when the company goes farther than what they initially thought, they need to re-evaluate the company. Of course, admitting they are wrong is not an easy thing for analysts to do as it isn't easy for anyone. However, when they do need to admit this, people can quickly learn what companies they should start paying attention to.

Earnings Momentum

While there are many important fundamental variables to look at when you are making an analysis, earnings momentum holds a special place. This variable is very important, especially when it comes to bull markets. Earnings momentum is the variable which looks at the year to year growth of earnings. Therefore, this is what will often set the price for stocks.

Strong Cash Flow

This is another fundamental variable that will tell you how much free cash a company has. This is a very important variable because it will let you know where a company financially sits after it has paid all of its bills and expenses. When you are getting into trading, you want to pay attention to the companies who are financially stable. You want to make sure that a company can grow because the more they grow, the more profit that you can make. Think about it – if you put your money into a stock where the company could barely pay the electric bill, do you think that your money would be secure, if even for a period of time? You want to make place your money in companies which are financially secure.

Earnings Growth

Another variable you want to pay attention to is how much more money the company is making as the years go on. When you look at this variable, you will be looking at the earnings growth variable. This is another company that you would think of investing in because you know that they have seen considerable growth for a certain number of years. Therefore, you analyze that the company will only continue to grow.

Chapter 12: Technical Analysis

Technical analysis is as important as fundamental analysis, especially when it comes to swing trading. However, you could view technical analysis as the more serious of the two types of analysis. Instead of just looking at the basics of the company and the fundamental variables which focus on your potential stock's company, you will focus more on the technical side of your stock when you look at technical analysis.

By definition, technical analysis is measuring the historical trends of the stock. Because many people feel that technical analysis is trickier than fundamental analysis, it might be wise to do more research about the topic before you start analyzing any stocks. There are a few online classes and books that are available for you, if you feel the need to become well educated on technical analysis.

One of the biggest factors to remember when you are focusing on technical analysis is you want to make sure to study every detail of your stock's history. You want to make sure you understand the trend, have made any notes you needed to, and that you believe you see the trend giving you the best profit before you decide to take on the stock. Technical analysis is going to take time and patience. However, you also don't want to spend too much time trying to decide if you want to take on a specific stock or not. This is a special time balance that you will figure out once have opened your account and on your way to trading stocks.

What You Will Study Through Technical Analysis

There are several details of the stock's history that you will look at when you are focusing on the technical analysis part of your trading schedule. This is something that you will do with every stock as it will help you decide if this stock is going to be worth your energy and time.

In order to give you a better view of what type of things you will look for, I will briefly discuss them below.

Study of Charts

Of course, one of the main pieces of the stock you will look at are the historical charts. These charts will give you some of the most detailed information that will help you make the best decision possible for your swing trading journey.

One of the most common charts are known as candlestick charts. These charts received this name because they are shaped like a candlestick. On top of that, the information you will find in the chart is designed through the candlestick. There are two main reasons why traders like candlestick charts so much. First, these charts are fairly easy to read and understand. Not only do they give you the information you need to know but they will also show off colors. The second reason is because these charts are known to give you an indication that the trend is about to change. For many people, this is extremely helpful because it decreases the amount of research that you need to do. However, there are other people that still say you should always perform your own research to make sure that the candlestick chart is correct on its assumption.

In general, the candlestick chart will tell you what the opening price was for the stock, the highest price, the lowest price, and the closing price. By getting these prices, you will start to analyze the chart to see what type of trend this stock is following. By looking at the history of the stock, you can start to get a sense of what the average prices are throughout the day. On top of this, you will also be able to get a sense of how much the stock tends to jump up and down during the day. On top of this, the candlestick chart will change colors in the center, depending on if the stock made a profit that day between the opening and closing price. For example, if the candlestick color is white or green, then you will know that the opening price was lower than the closing price. If you see a red or black color, then you will know that the opening price was higher than the closing price.

Of course, you will want to do this type of analysis for any chart that you come across, whether it is a line or pie chart. While each chart will look a bit different, they will all have the same valuable information within them. They will all tell you what the prices were throughout the day. However, not all of the charts will give you a prediction to what the trend will be doing next.

Volume

Another major part of technical analysis is the volume of a stock. The reasons why the volume is so important is because you will be able to get a sense of the intensity of the stock's movement in price. What this means is you will be able to take a certain amount of time, whether it is a few hours or a few months and get an idea of how many shares were traded during this time. Of course, the more shares that you find are traded, the better the stock is for trading. Stocks tend to reach high volume for many reasons. For example, they could be considered one of the more popular trading stocks on the market, such as Apple or Target. Another reason is because higher volume tends to mean a better profit. Think about it – people don't often take on trades where they are less likely to make a profit. Therefore, if the volume is high you know that most traders have found this stock to be successful.

Analyzing the Trend Line

I have already discussed a lot of information about trend lines in this book. By now, you should know that it is one of the main factors that will help you determine the success rate of a stock and whether you want to take on this stock or not. However, I feel it is important to mention that whenever you are analyzing a trend line, you are using technical analysis. You are not only analyzing what the trend line has done the previous day or the last couple of days, but you are most likely looking at the trend line over a period of months. The farther back you go, the more you will be able to learn details about the stock's trends.

Chapter 13: Managing Risk

One of the most important factors of any type of trading is learning how to manage risk. Of course, this is also one of the trickiest areas in this profession. While there are a lot of techniques and tips that can help you manage risk, you will never be able to completely eliminate risk. In fact, there is always some type of risk, no matter what stock you take on. You can decide to buy Amazon or Netflix, which are two of the best swing trading stocks on the market for 2019 and find yourself losing capital instead of gaining money. If this happens, it is simply because you didn't do everything you could at first to make sure that your risk was at a manageable level.

On top of this, you might have used the wrong strategy for the stock or not read the chart correctly. Remember, the prices of stocks are going up and down throughout the day. Furthermore, a downward spiral can find itself lower than the opening price of that day. Therefore, you always want to do what you can to make sure that you sell your stock at the correct time. If you find yourself losing money and realize you will probably be unable to make a profit, you will want to use your stop-loss strategy in order to get out of the trade as soon as possible as this will limit your loss.

How to Limit Your Risk

When it comes to trading in the stock market, it really doesn't matter what type of trading you are a part of, the ways to limit risk are generally the same. Most of them are pretty basic, and some have already been covered when I discussed some of the most common mistakes or tips for beginners. However, there are several that I didn't touch on, so I could give you some of the best ways to focus on limiting your risk in this chapter.

Keep Your Emotions in Check

While I have briefly touched on this before, I want to talk about making sure you can keep your emotions in check while trading in more detail. It is a very important factor to remember and once that can decrease your risk greatly.

One of the best examples to give you when it comes to the importance of keeping your emotions in check is the stock market crash of 1929. One of the reasons this crash occurred was because investors and traders started to let their emotions take over as they saw the stock market numbers decrease. How the numbers work is this way – when people are buying the stock, the price of the stock will increase. This also means that your profit is going up. However, when the price of the stock decreases, this means that people are selling.

Furthermore, it means that you are losing money. Therefore, when the people on the New York Stock Exchange in October saw the prices of stock dropping at a fast rate, most decided to quickly sell their stocks because they wanted to make sure they received as much profit as possible. On top of this, people were starting to fear what was going to happen to the stock market. Because of their emotions, they started to make irrational decisions about selling their stocks. Therefore, part of the reason for the stock market crash was because investors and traders let their emotions take over instead of focusing on thinking rationally.

The basis of controlling your emotions when it comes to making decisions in the stock market is to make sure you are making the most logical decision that you can. There is a lot of critical thinking that goes into deciding if you want to purchase or sell a stock. Many people can begin to feel overwhelmed, which can lead to a variety of negative emotions such as stress. When this happens, you are less likely to be able to think clearly, which is an important piece of critical thinking and keeping your emotions in check.

Furthermore, people can become greedy when they begin to see they are making a profit as a trader. Like with any other job, the more money people are making, the more money they want to receive. This is often a human reaction when it comes to money but it can also lead to people becoming greedy if this reaction is not kept in check. When traders become greedy, they start to look for the stocks that they believe will make the most money. When this happens, they are more likely to miss certain details about the stock, including the overall trend of the stock.

While trading is a stressful and exciting career, which are both strong emotions people feel, it is also a career that should not mix with your emotions. The less your emotions show as a trader, the more likely you will be to make sure you make the right decisions.

Keeping your emotions in check is especially important when you find a stock going against you. Not only does this make you realize that you made a mistake during your analysis and any calculations, which carries its own emotions, but this can also make you go through a series of emotional stages. There are many traders and investors who state that this series of five stages is similar to the five stages of grief. While some people feel that this is a bit over-dramatic, several experienced traders have discussed how they often feel these stages when they see a big loss from one of their stocks.

The five stages include:

1. Denial

When a trader reaches the stage of denial, they feel that they can't believe that the stock turned on them because it seemed like such as great move. Sometimes it takes the trader a while to realize that they are in a bad situation and about to lose a lot of money.

2. Anger

This is the stage where traders start to not only get mad at the stock market and other traders but also at themselves. While some will start to think that the stock market is against them, or blame the short sellers for their situations, other traders will become overly critical of themselves. During this time, they might become angry at themselves for not following their trading plan or for making a mistake.

3. Bargaining

The bargaining stage can occur before or right after they actually lose the money. While they have moved passed the first two stages, they still feel that there is something they can do. This is when some traders start trying to find a way out of the situation, such as asking God or another higher power to let them break even so they don't lose a huge amount of money.

4. Depression

At this point, traders will start to go over their plan and start to question what they did wrong. They start to feel depressed because they now realize that they have officially lost the money and there is no way to get the money back. They might start to dwell during this process and continue to become overly critical of themselves. However, instead of being angry, they might wonder why they didn't pay enough attention to their trading plan or the steps they were taking.

It is important to realize during this step that, unless a trader find himself in bad debt, he is most likely not in any type of clinical depression. While it is called depression, it is more like a sadness that can last anywhere from a couple of hours to a couple of days. However, if you do find yourself more in a depression because you ended up losing all of the money in your account and possibly still owe your broker, you might want to think of looking at counseling help. This is nothing to be ashamed about. In fact, there have been several traders who have found themselves in a depression because they sent themselves and their families into debt. As stated many times, trading can be a risky business and even some of the most experienced traders can make bad decisions that can cost them a lot of money.

5. Acceptance

This is the final step in the grief cycle. It is the step where while you might still be feeling a bit sad or a sense of guilt over losing so much money, but you accept that the situation has happened and close out your trade. You then do what you can to deal with the situation and continue on with your career. At this point, it is important to remember that just because you lost a lot of money doesn't mean you should end your trading career. As stated before, mistakes happen in the stock market. The best option you can do once you find yourself losing money is close out so you don't lose more money than you have to, learn from your mistake, and move on.

Follow the 1% Rule

One of the biggest ways to reduce your risk is to make sure that you focus on keeping your proportion low. One of the best ways to do this is to only risk about 1% of the money in your account with each trade. For example, if you have $10,000 in your account, this means that you will not trade more than $100 on a trade. However, many expert swing traders believe that when you are first starting out, you should lower this even more. Therefore, a beginner should look at trading no more than around 0.3% to 0.5%. While this doesn't seem like a lot of money, most stocks generally aren't a large amount of money to buy. Some of the most expensive stocks to buy will be blue-chip stocks.

Of course, there are always traders who often thrive on risk, which means that following the 1% rule won't feel comfortable to them. While this isn't advised for beginners, if you find yourself more comfortable taking higher risks, then you should think about increasing the percentage. For instance, instead of 1%, you could go up to 2% or 3%. However, it is not recommended that you go much higher than that. It really all depends on your personal preference with risk, your experience, and how much capital you have in your account.

One thing to think about before you decide on your percentage is how much capital you can lose if you find yourself in a losing streak. Think of it this way – if you have $25,000 in your account (which is often minimum) and you find yourself putting 2% of your capital into a couple of different trades that you lose on both, you are going to find yourself losing a lot of money quickly. While you can always add more money into your account every time, you can easily see how this can affect your finances.

On top of that, losing can affect a person psychologically, especially when you are losing money. People generally take losing money more seriously than losing a lot of other things. Part of this is because we are so dependent on money. We need money to pay for our home, our vehicles, groceries, and other bills. Furthermore, we need money to purchase the things we want, including stocks. Therefore, when you find your amount of capital decreasing rapidly in your account, you're going to start feeling affected psychologically, which is going to affect you emotionally. Of course, this can cause a whole new set of problems when it comes to trading, as we have already discussed.

Determine a Stop-Loss Amount

However, just how can you determine the right proportion size for your account? There are actually factors that can help you with this. After you have looked at setting your risk at 1%, you can look at another factor, which is setting your trade risk. This is when you set your stop-loss amount. This amount will be created when you set up your trading plan. For example, if you spent $10.00 on your trade, then you might set up your stop-loss level at $9.80. This means that once you reach this amount, you will sell that stock and only lose .20 cents. Most traders will look at the percentage of their account they put towards their stock in order to help them determine their stop-loss amount. This is because some traders might feel more comfortable setting their stop-loss amount at a higher percentage if they followed the 1% rule than a if they decided to go up to 3% or even 5%.

Follow Your Guidelines and Rules

We have already discussed various way to help you eliminate risk when we discussed some of the common mistakes and various tips for beginners. These are important to follow as they will help you eliminate risk. For example, making sure you stay in the right mindset will help you remain positive about trading. This can help you eliminate your risk because you will continue to put your best effort into making sure that you make the best decisions when it comes to your trades.

As you get started in your trading career, you will start to develop your own rules and guidelines, such as in your trading plan. It is important that you don't change any of these rules and guidelines without fully looking at your trade as a whole. On top of this, it is important to follow because it will help keep you focused, you will begin to learn the details of swing trading easier as you won't be so concerned about your next step, and you will feel more comfortable in your abilities.

Don't Trade Alone

Earlier I discussed the importance of finding a broker as they will not only help you with your trades, but they will also advise you through your swing trading career. This is especially important for beginners as it is a great way to lower your risk. There is a lot you will still learn as you start to trade. Even when you begin trading with

261

simulations, which means you don't use real money, to get a feel of what trading in the stock market is really like; you will still feel different once you start using real money. Therefore, it is important to make sure that you have someone you trust that you can bring your questions, concerns, and can help teach you how to manage your account and all the other facts that go into trading.

Of course, this doesn't mean that you always need a broker. In fact, there are a lot of swing traders who don't have brokers. However, at first, you should always make sure that you have someone to help guide you until you learn the world of swing trading a little better and become more comfortable making decisions on your own. For example, you might have a broker for the first couple of years you are a swing trader and then decide that you are content with making your own decisions.

It's important to note that just because swing traders don't have a broker doesn't mean they don't get advice or information from other traders to help them along in their career. Every swing trader will tell you that no matter where you are in your career or how comfortable you are with trading, you should always be a part of an online forum. Even if you decide to create your own swing trading forum one day, you will still continue to communicate with people who will help you along your swing trading journey. This is important as the people you find in your online communities will start to become similar to your co-workers. Having people who have similar interests and understand the factors that go into the job, such as the risk, stress, level of commitment, and excitement will help you remain successful in your career. They will help you stick to the right mindset.

Chapter 14: The Psychology of

Swing Trading

Many traders would never imagine that there is psychology in the world of swing trading. However, if you think about it, there is a lot of psychology in trading. In fact, you wouldn't be able to trade or become a successful trader if you didn't include psychology in the field. Not only do you use psychology when you are analyzing your research and information, but you also use psychology when you are focusing on your winning mindset and making sure you are mentally healthy.

In general, psychology is the study of the mind. While this might seem like a strange thing to include when trading, if you think about it, you are always critically thinking when you are working as a trader. You are always thinking about the charts you are seeing, you are always observing what is going on around you, so you can make note on the conditions of the stock market and your environment for your trading journal. On top of this, you are analyzing yourself as a trader, so you can become the best swing trader possible. All of this requires using the mind to analyze, which is basically studying the mind. However, instead of studying someone else's mind as psychologists usually do, you are studying your own mind.

One of the biggest ways psychology becomes a part of swing trading is by teaching you to analyze the reports and charts you see on a daily basis. Through analyzing the ways in which the stock market prices go up and down, the closing price, and the opening price you are able to piece together an average price. On top of this, as you continue to analyze the charts by going back in history to look at previous days and then analyze the general conditions of the stock market, you will be able to start to note what direction the stock is going to take. You will start to see a pattern and you will be able to think about where the pattern is going to go next to see if you should invest in this stock or not.

Another huge way psychology is a part of trading is through your trading journal. Whether you use charts and make notes, write in a journal, or both you will be writing down various pieces of information that will help you look at yourself as a trader. Through this, you will be able to see what your strengths are, what your weaknesses are, where you tend to feel the most stress, and what you still need to research when it comes to the stock market. Without being able to analyze yourself, you wouldn't be able to figure out all this information to help you become a successful trader.

Finally, psychology has a lot to do with your mental health. While I have discussed this, it is important to take time to explain how this ties into psychology. The easiest way to think about this is by realizing that your peace of mind, which is your ability to remain calm so you don't become stressed and then allow other emotions to creep up and influence your decision-making is tied to trading results. In fact, these factors are all tied to your trading results.

When you are doing well – you are not only making a good amount of profit, but you are limiting your mistakes and are completing your daily tasks, you begin to feel confident in your abilities. When this happens, you start to feel happier, you start to feel more relaxed, and you start to become more determined. In fact, many experienced traders have stated that the more confident you are in your abilities as a trader, the more determined you will be. This will help you because you will start to focus more on your responsibilities and begin to perform better overall.

When you are doing poorly – you are seeing more capital loss than capital gains, you are making more mistakes, and you are having trouble completing your daily tasks, you begin to feel poorly. Not only does your mental health start to decline, but you will stop paying attention to what you eat. You won't get enough sleep and, overall, you will stop taking care of yourself as well as you do when you are mentally healthy. All these factors will affect your trading results. You won't perform as well as you did when your mental health was stronger.

Because most people don't think of this, it is important to note. You need to realize that your energy level, alertness, confidence, and overall health (mental, emotional, and physical) will affect your trading results. Because of this, in order to become the best trader that you can be, you want to make sure you are doing everything you can in order to increase your mental health. The best benefit of doing this is that you will not only find yourself handling your swing trading career better, but you will also feel better in your personal life. In fact, making sure you are in an overall healthy state will help you in all areas of your life.

At this point, it is important to note that no matter how you mentally feel, everyone has some improvement to work on mentally. If you begin to realize that you are overly critical of yourself, you lack confidence, or you struggle in other ways, you are not alone. You can further work to improve your mental health in a variety of ways so you can become a successful swing trader.

Maintain Your Mental Health

There are dozens of ways to help you maintain your mental health. I won't be able to cover them all in this book, but I will focus on several to give yourself different techniques to choose from so you can help build up your mental health.

Make Sure You Get Enough Sleep

Many people do not understand how not getting enough sleep can affect your mental health. In fact, in can affect it in more than one way. First, when you don't get enough sleep, you are just not as alert as you should be. When this happens, your mental health is affected because it doesn't feed off your positive emotions as it should. It's not that being less alert makes you depressed, it is simply that your body is trying to conserve energy, therefore, your mind doesn't receive the energy it needs to keep your mental state healthy.

Another way not getting enough sleep can affect your mental health is by giving up on tasks easier. Because you are tired and sluggish, you don't have the energy to deal with your regular daily tasks. This can have a downfall on your mental health. Instead of feeling like you are accomplishing your tasks, you begin to feel like you are wasting your time and that you won't be able to complete your tasks successfully. Of course, this can make you feel less confident in your abilities. While feeling like this rarely won't affect your mental health much in the long term, it can in the short term. On top of this, if you get in the habit of not getting enough sleep, you will find your mental health decreasing rapidly.

Focus on the Positive

One of the biggest ways to boost your mental health is to focus on the positive. While there are many negative things that are going to happen to you on a daily basis, it is important to make sure that you focus on the positive things that happen. For example, if you accomplish a task, take a moment to reflect on this task and be proud of your accomplishment. This will not only help boost your self-esteem, but it will also help you get rid of any negativity you were feeling.

Practice Self-Control

Self-control is an important factor when it comes to trading and mental health. When it comes to trading, you want to make sure you are practicing self-control because you will become more likely to accomplish the tasks you need to, stick to your schedule, and follow any techniques, strategies, and tips that you are given so you can become a successful trader.

When it comes to mental health, it is important to practice self-control because you will be better able to control your thoughts. You can train your mind, in a sense, to focus more on the positive. For example, many psychologists will give their clients who focus on the negative a task. This task simply states that for any negative thought they have they need to replace it with two positive thoughts.

Conclusion

Congratulations for making it to the end of this book! I know it was a lot of information for you to take in, so this is really an accomplishment in your swing trading career!

One of the goals of this book was to give you a start on your swing trading career. Not only did I want to explain the key concepts of financial trading. Because this is considered to be a foundation when it comes to trading, I didn't want to leave this information out of the book. On top of this, it was important to explain to you the difference between trading and investing. There are a lot of people who get into trading when they believed they were going to be investing money instead of trading stocks in order to gain a profit. Because these two topics are different, it is important to make sure you want to be a trader and not an investor before you go too far into your research for swing trading.

Another major point of this book was to give you a concise beginner's guide about swing trading which touched on a variety of topics. Instead of you having to read dozens more articles and a few books about swing trading, I wanted to give you a way that you can place one book in your device to turn to when you need a refresher about swing trading. On top of this, I wanted you to be able to bring this book to your friends who are interested in swing trading and show them this beginner's guide, so they can get all the information required before opening their account with a broker.

As you have realized by this point, swing trading is not the easiest career; however, when it comes to the stock market, there is no easy career. It doesn't matter if you decide on swing trading, become a buy and hold investor, or get into day trading you will find that each one of these areas have their own challenges. However, you will soon come to find that they each have their own advantages as well. You should already to be able to pick out a few advantages to becoming a swing trader. For example, you could one day be able to trade without the assistance of a broker. On top of this, you have been able to get a sneak peak of the many online communities for swing traders. Once you decide to join an online community or two, you will realize how enjoyable swing trading is.

You should also understand what simulation trading is and how important it is to make sure you complete this type of trading before you start trading for money. You should also not only understand risks which are associated in swing trading but also have an idea on how to decrease these risks once you start swing trading. Of course, this is one reason you want to make sure to practice simulation trading at first. As stated before, simulation trading will help you make sure that you understand the risks and the strategies which are associated with swing trading.

By now you should not only clearly understand what swing trading is, but also what the average time fame is for a swing trader. You should be able to remember the 11 commandments of swing trading, techniques, what the right mindset is when you are trading, know a variety of tips to help you get on your way, and also understand the many mistakes that other swing traders have made.

Furthermore, you should be able to explain how a day will go for a full-time swing trader, be able to explain the two different types of stock market conditions, and the art of short selling.

On top of all the information you need to know about being a swing trader, you also know how to get started with researching as much information as possible. On top of this, you have learned tips to help you become a better researcher, so you can gain the most out of your research time. It is important to keep these tips in mind as you will need to used them throughout your career. On top of this, you can also add your own tips, which will become useful when you begin to help other

CPSIA information can be obtained
at www.ICGtesting.com
Printed in the USA
LVHW010917180520
655781LV00004B/232

9 781951 652265